COMMANDERS OF THE DINING ROOM

SOUTHERN FOODWAYS ALLIANCE
STUDIES IN CULTURE, PEOPLE, AND PLACE

The series explores key themes and tensions in food studies—including race, class, gender, power, and the environment—on a macroscale and also through the microstories of men and women who grow, prepare, and serve food. It presents a variety of voices, from scholars to journalists to writers of creative nonfiction.

SERIES EDITOR

John T. Edge

COMMANDERS
of the
DINING ROOM

BIOGRAPHIC SKETCHES
AND PORTRAITS OF
SUCCESSFUL HEAD WAITERS

E. A. Maccannon

Foreword by Maurice Carlos Ruffin
With a New Introduction by Danya M. Pilgrim

The University of Georgia Press

ATHENS

Paperback edition published in 2021 by
the University of Georgia Press
Additional materials © 2021 by the University of Georgia Press
Athens, Georgia 30602
www.ugapress.org
All rights reserved

Most University of Georgia Press titles are
available from popular e-book vendors.

Printed digitally

Library of Congress Cataloging-in-Publication Data
Names: Maccannon, E. A., author.
Title: Commanders of the dining room : biographic sketches and portraits of successful head waiters / by E. A. Maccannon ; foreword by Maurice Carlos Ruffin with a new introduction by Danya Pilgrim.
Description: Athens, Georgia : The University of Georgia Press, [2021] | Series: Southern foodways alliance studies in culture, people, and place ; 12
Identifiers: LCCN 2021029510 (print) | LCCN 2021029511 (ebook) |
ISBN 9780820360805 | ISBN 9780820360799 (epub)
Subjects: LCSH: Waiters—Biography.
Classification: LCC TX910.3.M33 2021 (print) | LCC TX910.3 (ebook) |
DDC 642/.6092 [B]—dc23
LC record available at https://lccn.loc.gov/2021029510
LC ebook record available at https://lccn.loc.gov/2021029511

Originally published in 1904 by the Gwendolyn Publishing Company

CONTENTS

Foreword to the 2021 Edition vii

Introduction to the 2021 Edition xiii

Introduction 1

History of the Founding of the HSWNBA 5

Frank P. Thompson 13

W. Alonza Locke 17

Edward W. Harper 19

E. C. Holland 25

Thomas J. Simons 27

Robert H. Grant 31

Thomas A. Morris 35

C. C. Randolph 37

H. Pettigrew 43

A. E. Jenkins 45

Walter C. Outlow 49

W. P. Landon 53

Calvin M. Farrar 55

Geo. A. Curry 57

Richard Jones Wilder 61

John A. Gloster 65

W. R. Harris 69

James L. Dickerson 71

J. T. Lee 73

William S. Foreman 77

J. H. Holmes 81

George H. Richardson 83

Albert L. Waiters	85
L. D. Houston	87
John T. Gilbert	91
John C. Logan	93
Sam Randle Wilson	97
Charles T. Ferguson	99
Thomas A. Wood	101
C. B. Coles	105
Harvey C. Green	109
Chas C. Smith	111
Wm. E. Tucker	113
Thomas C. Smith	117
John T. Stanton	121
A. C. Pitts	123
Jas. H. Whitehead	127
Nicholas C. Johns	129
William A. Fisher	131
A. Nathaniel Dempsey	133
J. J. Miles	135
Thomas Frazier	139
Samuel Thompson	141
George P. Goode	143
Edward F. Mathews	145
A. H. Dailey	149
Frank C. Long	151
Marion M. Martin	155
F. H. Griffin	157
R. J. Patterson	159
Edward W. Diggs	161
W. Forrest Cozart	163

FOREWORD TO THE REISSUE
by Maurice Carlos Ruffin

The problem these men faced was obvious. Though they had the good fortune to live up north during the collapse of Reconstruction, they were losing work. It was a fact of their time. In fine restaurants from Washington, D.C. to Chicago, Black head waiters were being replaced by white head waiters. Some of these actions were thought to stem from the idea that white head waiters were naturally better, more cultured, and efficient in their practices. But this was the tail end of the 1890s, the Progressive Era, a time of political activism aimed at rooting out crooked politicians and bringing voting rights to the disenfranchised. This was a time when ordinary people took nothing lying down.

On September 20, 1899, a group of men came together at Bethel AME Church in Chicago's so-called Black Belt. Just a few blocks from Lake Michigan, this was the magnet that attracted so many southern Blacks during the Great Migration, the future home of the first Black-owned bank in Illinois, the Binga Bank, and the neighborhood Ida B. Wells moved to after threats on her life in reply to her investigative journalism on lynching.

The convention at Bethel church was led by W. Forrest Cozart and Joseph B. Goins. Along with one hundred others gathered there, they formed the Head and Second Waiters National Benefit Association (HSWNBA, hereinafter "The Waiters" for our purposes). You've no doubt heard of benefit associations: the famed Zulu Social Aid and Pleasure Club in New Orleans, still extant today, is an example of one. Such clubs came together, in part, to cover funeral expenses for deceased community members and to support surviving family. The Waiters had an additional specific goal. To stem the job losses among their membership.

Their solution was straight forward—train their members to be the very best Head and Second Waiters they could be. To modern eyes, this may seem like a laughably modest solution. Indeed, the Waiters acknowledged as much in one of the profiles:

> In the years and generations to come such a worthy progress as we chronicle above, might seem insignificant when compared to the heights of successive achievements to which the progenies of his kindred shall have ascended; but then the natural acorn of ability which is found in such men as Mr. Morris and many others in various other callings, will have a more fertile field and a freer atmosphere in which to grow and develop into the world's giant oak. (p. 44)

If the Waiters were aware that their goals were small, even uninspiring, why not aim higher? Why not work for new legislation or take to the streets in protest?

We must remind ourselves that much of the history of Black resistance is that of the slingshot versus the giant. Many Black leaders have made the calculation to ask for less than they may have thought their community was entitled. Civil Rights Movement activists of the 1960s didn't ask for the full rights that most Americans enjoyed. After decades of struggle, they procured the right to vote as well as workplace and school protections, both circumscribed by various caveats. The Black Lives Matter movement hasn't argued that Black lives are better than white lives, let alone equal to white lives; they've merely suggested that Black Lives are more than insignificant. The movement has been met with significant pushback. Time after time, Black communities have questioned why they aren't guaranteed the same constitutional rights afforded to most Americans. Time after time, Black communities have been cautioned to wait, to remain silent, to make do.

Cozart and Goins, who were elected Chairman and Secretary of the Waiters, respectively, rose to prominence more than one hundred twenty years ago. Their work predates the 1939 Alexandria library sit-in, the wade-in at Biloxi beach in 1959, and the early 1960s sit-ins of Greensboro, Nashville, Baltimore, and Wichita.

In 1917, white laborers killed as many as two hundred fifty Black workers in East St. Louis. The Black community responded with the Silent Parade, ten thousand people who didn't say a word so that others might hear, marching through New York City, the first such protest of its kind (a bigger Silent Parade in Newark, New Jersey followed in 1918). But Cozart and Goins and the Waiters came before all that, too. Booker T. Washington had only just struck the 1895 Atlanta Compromise, in which he promised white southern leaders that Blacks would not fight for equality, integration, or justice so long as they were allowed *some* education and *some* due process.

Cozart and Goins were men of my great-great grandparents' generation: born into slavery, promised a kind of freedom, but ultimately offered a second-class citizenship, which still endures in the present day.

Working from such a low position, it seems unfair for modern observers to malign the Waiters for seeking small gains. After all, the Waiters and other African Americans achieved significant political and economic gains during the period between emancipation and the advent of Jim Crow despite massive, sometimes deadly, resistance. What they lacked in modern radical vision, they made up for with practical contemporary determination. The Waiters carried on with their plan, though they suffered their fair share of tumult. The D.C. attendees stormed out of the very first convention after refusing to contribute to the general fund (they would return in a subsequent meeting).

The Waiters also found successes. Perhaps their greatest triumph occurs in the pages of this book, in the presentation of the members, their lives, their accomplishments. On some level, the minds of people who commit racist acts are infested with a belief in the inhumanity, inferiority, and insignificance of Black people. This is why so many Black activists and thought leaders played what today some call Respectability Politics. If one convinces their detractors that they are better than their detractors think they are, then gains will be made: that is respectability politics at work.

More context is needed to understand the Waiters' tactics. In the wake of Frederick Douglass's death, Booker T. Washington arguably became the leading Black voice in America. Washington toured the country giving impassioned speeches to large crowds. His message was as direct as it was popular. Forget about fighting racist policies. Never mind tearing down the unjust system. Washington argued Black people could achieve equality by working to educate themselves. Personal improvement was the key to the future.

The Waiters modestly sought to improve themselves. The leaders of the association understood that the standards of fine dining had been set in Europe and adopted by the best restaurants in America. By learning those standards and adopting them as their own, Waiters could eliminate what they believed to be a primary reason for their declining employment rates.

The Waiters also knew that being a professional waiter was about more than great table service. A respected head or second waiter needed a reputation. One of the ways they burnished their reputations was through the book you hold in your hands. The profiles in this book present many of the Waiters' origins, personalities, and work histories.

Many of profiles take a similar form. The subject is identified as someone from humble origins. He was born into slavery, which deprived him of a chance to train himself in the ways of American professional culture. However, he was industrious and hard-working. Those attributes helped Waiters find employment at often small, unassuming restaurants. In the process, they learned the basics of the service industry, which meant they were ready when better opportunities became available. Invariably, they were hired at respected establishments as second or side waiters. After a period of years or decades, they were elevated to the top position where they thrived and proved their value to the business.

What may strike readers most about the Waiters in the present book is their hopefulness. Anyone alive today with an understanding of racial strife in America knows that, even in the twenty-first century, something is not quite right. During the years between the time of the Waiters and now, untold numbers of Black Americans have been deprived of their rights, brutalized, and killed. One might argue that the Waiters efforts haven't amounted to much in the final analysis. To those people, I offer a challenge of the imagination. Imagine a world where no one stood up for the rights of Black Americans. It took centuries of opposition to undo the foul institution of slavery, to upend Jim Crow, to secure voting rights, to open fair housing, to reduce redlining, to roll back predatory lending. There are many battles still to be fought and won in the arenas of policing, mass incarceration, drug policy, & many others. If those injustices are ever to be relegated to the scrapheap of history, it falls on dedicated, moral Americans to take whatever steps they can wherever they are in life. All Americans owe a debt of gratitude to the men in this book for the goodness in their hearts.

INTRODUCTION
TO THE 2021 EDITION

Edwin A. Maccannon, born around 1866 in St. Kitts, British West Indies, disembarked in New York from the *Creole* in the spring of 1884.[1] The trim young man joined the teeming throng of migrants pouring into the United States. Black Caribbean migration, although small in scale compared to the influx of European migrants, had an important impact on African American communities. By 1900 about twenty thousand of the almost nine million people who made up the Black population in the United States were foreign born. By 1910, more than half of the foreign-born Black population traced their path back to the British West Indies and Cuba.[2]

Upon arrival, one of Maccannon's first tasks would have been finding employment. During what historian Rayford Logan termed the nadir of race relations and during a run of financial depressions at the end of the nineteenth century, men and women of African descent faced increasingly aggressive tactics designed to limit their employment opportunities. For a young man like Maccannon one of the most accessible jobs would have been that of waiter.[3] By mid-century, native-born white men had begun to consider waiting tables menial labor and avoided such service work whenever possible, but neither white European migrants nor Black men had the luxury of turning away from positions as waiters.

Early in the nineteenth century, Black men took the job of waiter and transformed it into an occupation that, when mastered, could lead to better prospects and upward class mobility.[4] For Black men, being a waiter did not preclude them from attaining middle-class status, becoming community leaders, and leading activist lives. Black men and women insisted that waiting was not menial work but could be respectable and dignified.

Robert Roberts who published *The House Servant's Directory* in 1827, Tunis Campbell who published the *Hotel Keepers, Head Waiters, and Housekeepers' Guide* in 1848, and John B. Goins who published *The American Colored Waiter* in 1902, provided top-notch instruction for would-be waiters, backed by their own practical experience. Roberts, Campbell, and Goins assured their readers that attention to the minute details of the job, carried out with decorum, would bring them respect, steady employment, and additional rewards. While Black people fought to open doors in other industries, they counted on waiting to provide either temporary work or a long-term livelihood.

The hierarchy of the hospitality industry meant that many men began their careers as errand boys, bellboys, scullions, dish carriers, and silver washers, before working their way into positions as waiters. In addition to taking orders and serving guests, waiters might also be assigned duties such as washing windows, mopping floors, and preparing relishes.[5] Ambitious waiters sought to rise to the post of second waiter or captain. These men served as an extension of the head waiter, carrying out all his instructions while having charge over a set number of waiters in the dining room.

The head waiter oversaw every element of the dining room, from ambiance to service, while marshaling waiters and managing guests. The proprietor of the establishment counted on the head waiter to run an operation on schedule and up to standard. Truly, they were the commanders and superintendents that Maccannon described. The head waiter exemplified dignity, diplomacy, and efficiency. Jessup Whitehead, a white author of instructional books for the hospitality industry, described the head waiter as "always a man of respectable appearance, sometimes quite a superior man in this respect, and . . . fairly well dressed. His manner is polite and his speech soft; it is his business to be attentive and appear solicitous for the comfort of the guests." Whitehead further recognized the head waiter as a "king-maker" who had the power to build up or tear down the reputation of an establishment and its workers. While Maccannon also described the role of the head waiter in maintaining "proper order" in the dining room, he emphasized the intelligence, education, skillfulness, and sterling character of Black head waiters.[6]

Despite the long history of able work performed by Black waiters, hotel and resort restaurant owners gravitated toward hiring European migrants in the last quarter of the nineteenth century. Even if employers did not consider them white by the social lexicon of the day, European migrants, at least, appeared phenotypically white, had a passing familiarity with the European plan adopted by many hotels in the United States, and could be hired at low wages.[7] Most hospitality establishments located outside of the South hired interracial staffs.[8] Although race sometimes kept them separate, waiters and other food service workers also realized that their interests could bring them together.

Labor action in the United States increased over the end of the nineteenth century. Founded in 1869 the Knights of Labor, over time, admitted both Black people and women to the organization. The Knights reached their peak of 700,000 official members in 1886, just after Maccannon migrated to the United States.[9] Internal issues and failed strikes led to their decline. Many workers left the broad-based coalition for organizations that focused on their unique occupational concerns. The Culinary Alliance, founded in 1889 by German service workers in Chicago, was such an organization.

The leadership of the Alliance pondered the issue of strikebreaking as they planned a protest for the spring of 1890. Recognizing that employers often turned to local and Southern Black men to keep their doors open during labor actions, organizers began meeting with African American groups to forestall that possibility. The Alliance built a coalition of labor organizations, each made up of a singular race or ethnicity. This enabled them to threaten business owners with the possibility that African Americans would strike at the same time as their white colleagues. In using the specter of race for their own aims, white

Alliance leaders secured the recognition of their organization as well as a pay raise, but the proprietors continued to refuse the demand to hire only union men.[10]

The union made good on their threat, and African American waiters got the full support of the Culinary Alliance when they walked out of downtown Chicago restaurants during the busy lunch hour on May 8, 1890. By creating a biracial leadership board that operated on a principle of equality and by organizing restaurant as well as hotel and private club workers, the Culinary Alliance and the Black waiters brought their strike to a successful conclusion.[11]

White and Black waiters shared many complaints, however African American waiters also had unique problems intensified by racialized thinking. While white hotel waiters might make up to thirty dollars a month and work about twelve hours a day, Black waiters might make less than twenty-five dollars a month and work fifteen to sixteen hours a day. Tipping became increasingly important to Black waiters because employers refused to provide them with a living wage. Providing a high level of service to get a tip, and to increase the amount of that tip, proved problematic.

John Gilmer Speed echoed popular opinion in a 1902 *Lippincott's Magazine*, stating that Black men's desire for tips was "a token of their inferiority...Tips go with servility, and no man who is a voter in this country by birthright is in the least justified in being in service."[12] Speed did not address the fact that Black men were kept, intentionally and often violently, from entering other occupations, or that they were paid less than white men for more work.

Previous interracial coalitions broke down in 1903 when white waiters refused to support their Black colleagues and pushed aggressively for a segregated organization. This paved the way for employers to push Black men out of their waiter positions, to hire white men, and increasingly, white women.[13] It was in this context that W. Forrest Cozart and John B. Goins began working on the Head and Second Waiters National Benefit Association (HSWNBA).

The HSWNBA formed a keystone connecting nineteenth-century and twentieth-century organizing efforts. From the convention movement founded in 1830 to the National Association for the Advancement of Colored People formed in 1909 to the Brotherhood of Sleeping Car Porters and Maids founded in 1925, Black people across the country gathered in societies, leagues, and unions to realize one goal: the full inclusion of African Americans in the social, cultural, civic, and economic life of the nation.

A host of Black community organizations supported the growth of the HSWNBA. Black newspapers such as the *Indiana Freeman* carried a column entitled "The Waiter" edited by Cozart. The column provided advice and instruction for waiters, celebrated those who had secured head waiter positions, and noted those who were changing jobs. Cozart also mentioned places that would not hire Black waiters. Black churches and clubs opened their doors for the HSWNBA to hold meetings and conventions. Black publishers produced books and magazines such as *The Waiters', Hotel Bellmen, and Railroad Porters' Journal*. In 1904 Edwin A. Maccannon, then proprietor of the Gwendolyn Publishing Company, featured the HSWNBA's most august members in a collection of biographies, *Commanders of the Dining Room*. You now hold a facsimile of that book in your hand.

Maccannon published *Commanders* to increase the visibility and stature of Black waiters; to assure employers that they could count on members of the HSWNBA to thoroughly know their business; to attest to their commitment to be dependable workers who would not create labor unrest; and to showcase model African American manhood. *Commanders* joined works like *Men of Mark, Eminent, Progressive and Rising* to provide proof of Black progress, intellect, and success through portraiture and biography.[14] These books provided convincing counternarratives to denigrating portrayals of Black people, and Black men in particular. *Commanders* proclaimed to young waiters that they could achieve success if they educated themselves, worked hard, and joined an association like the HSWNBA. In *Commanders* they could see headwaiters, at the pinnacle of the profession, who had once started out at the bottom and worked their way to the top, overcoming a variety of challenges along the way.

Scholars have used Maccannon's work in studies of the hospitality industry, but also in performance studies, literary history, labor history, and in local studies of Black communities.[15] Maccannon's *Commanders* is an elastic text that should prove valuable beyond its most obvious uses. Specialists in visual culture will find the photographs a compelling study. *Commanders* might provide turn-of-the-twentieth-century context to Black masculinity studies and to studies on class. The details of the places where head waiters worked could expand the source base for researchers of Black geography, mobility, and migration.

Maccannon's *Commanders of the Dining Room* places us in the intriguing world of early twentieth-century head waiters. Their brief biographies compel us to think about the ways in which histories of labor, class, gender, migration, and race inform one another, just as they did in Maccannon's life. Maccannon and his wife Annie, both Black West Indian migrants, made a home for their family in the United States. Although he eventually relinquished the publishing business, Maccannon remained in Brooklyn. Both he and his wife are buried there in Evergreen Cemetery.[16]

Though times have changed, those who work in the food and hospitality industry today still face many of the same issues around tipping and low wages. More, they continue to face a lack of appreciation and regard for the challenging work they do. To paraphrase Maccannon, should their work not endear them to everyone who enjoys the luxuries of American dining rooms? Should they not receive the respect and recognition they are due?

Danya M. Pilgrim

NOTES

1. Maccannon's migration documents record that he was five foot two and weighed 120 pounds. National Archives and Records Administration; Washington, D.C.; NAI Title: Index to Petitions for Naturalizations Filed in Federal, State, and Local Courts in New York City, 1792–1906; NAI Number: 5700802; Record Group Title: Records of District Courts of the United States, 1685–2009; Record Group Number: RG 21. Ancestry.

2. *The American Negro, His History and Literature: Negro Population in the United States, 1790–1915* (New York: Arno Press and the New York Times, 1968), 61–63. Google Books. These figures exclude Puerto Rico.

3. Margaret Garb, "The Great Chicago Waiters' Strike: Producing Urban Space, Organizing Labor, Challenging Racial Divides in 1890s Chicago," *Journal of Urban History* 40, no. 6 (November 2014): 1086. doi:10.1177/0096144214536864.

4. See Kelly Erby, *Restaurant Republic: the Rise of Public Dining in Boston* (Minneapolis: University of Minnesota Press, 2016); Erby, "Worthy of Respect; Black Waiters in Boston Before the Civil War," *Food and History* 5, no. 2 (2007): 205–17; Rafia Zafar, "Recipes for Respect: Black Hospitality Entrepreneurs Before World War I," in *African American Foodways*, ed. Anne L. Bower (Urbana: University of Illinois Press, 2007), 139–52; Danya M. Pilgrim, "Masters of a Craft: Philadelphia's Black Public Waiters, 1820–50," *Pennsylvania Magazine of History and Biography* 142, no. 3 (October 2018): 269–293.

5. John B. Goins, *The American Waiter* (Chicago: Hotel Monthly Press, 1908), 3.

6. Jessup Whitehead, *The Steward's Handbook and Guide to Party Catering* (Chicago: J. Whitehead & Co., 1903), 19. HathiTrust; E. A. Maccannon, *Commanders of the Dining Room* (New York: Gwendolyn Publishing Co., 1904), 10.

7. Cindy Lobel, "'Out to Eat': the Emergence and Evolution of the Restaurant in Nineteenth-Century New York City," *Winterthur Portfolio* 44, no. 2/3 (2010): 200. doi:10.1086/654885; Goins, 123–127. European plan meals were served a la carte and the price was not included in the cost of accommodation. For discussion of the ways in which different European immigrant groups became racialized as white see David Roediger, *The Wages*

of Whiteness: Race and the Making of the American Working Class (London and New York: Verso Books, 1991) and *Working Towards Whiteness: How America's Immigrants Became White: the Strange Journey from Ellis Island to the Suburbs* (New York: Basic Books, 2005), Noel Ignatiev, *How the Irish Became White* (New York: Routledge, 1995), Matthew Frye Jacobson, *Whiteness of a Different Color: European Immigrants and the Alchemy of Race* (Cambridge: Harvard University Press, 1999), and Thomas Guglielmo, *White on Arrival: Italians, Race, Color, and Power in Chicago, 1890–1945* (Oxford University Press, 2003).

8. Garb, 1085.

9. Matthew Hild, "The Knights of Labor in Arkansas: a Research Note," *Arkansas Historical Quarterly* 79, no. 1 (Spring 2020):59. ProQuest.

10. Garb, 1079–1083.

11. Ibid, 1082,1088.

12. John Gilmer Speed, "Tips and Commissions," *Lippincott's Magazine* 69 (1902):78.

13. Garb, 1091–1092.

14. William J. Simmons, *Men of Mark: Eminent, Progressive and Rising* (Cleveland: Geo. M. Revell & Co., 1887). Documenting the American South.

15. See Christopher Robert Reed, *Black Chicago's First Century, vol. 1 1833–1900* (Columbia: University of Missouri Press, 2005); Andrew Haley, *Turning the Tables: Restaurants and the Rise of the American Middle Class 1880–1920* (Chapel Hill: University of North Carolina Press, 2011); Jerry Dickey, "African American Waiters and Cakewalk Contests in Florida East Coast Resorts of the Gilded Age," in *Working in the Wings: New Perspectives on Theatre History and Labor*, ed. Elizabeth A. Osbourne and Christine Woodworth (Carbondale: Southern Illinois University Press, 2015), 125–138; Luke Mielke, "Racial Uplift in a Jim Crow Local: Black Union Organizing in Minneapolis Hotels 1930–1940," American Studies Honor Thesis (Macalester College, 2016); Christoph Ribbat, "Waiters, Writers, and Power: From Dining Room Commanders to the Emotional Proletariat," in *Food, Power, and Agency*, ed. Jurgen Martschukat and Bryant Simon (New York: Bloomsbury Academic, 2017), 59–82; Sally E. Svenson, *Blacks in the Adirondacks* (New York: Syracuse University Press, 2017).

16. Maccannon married Annie Waters in 1896. Waters, also from St. Kitts, migrated to the United States in 1888. By 1904 Maccannon, who held several jobs, became a publisher working out of 130 Fulton Street in New York.

He made his home with Annie and their children at the time in Brooklyn. Maccannon and Annie remained in Brooklyn until her death in 1931 and his in 1955. Year: 1900; Census Place: Brooklyn Ward 24, Kings, New York; Page: 12; Enumeration District: 0424; FHL microfilm: 1241062; Year: 1910; Census Place: Brooklyn Ward 26, Kings, New York; Roll: T624_979; Page: 15A; Enumeration District: 0983; FHL microfilm: 1374992; Ancestry.com. New York, New York, Extracted Marriage Index, 1866–1937 [database on-line]. Provo, Utah, USA: Ancestry.com Operations, Inc., 2014; *Trow's General Directory of the Boroughs of Manhattan and Bronx, City of New York for the Year Ending July 1, 1905* (New York: Trow Directory, Printing and Bookbinding Co., 1905), 836.

COMMANDERS OF THE DINING ROOM

INTRODUCTION.

In publishing this work of biographic sketches and portraits of successful head waiters of America, it is with the full confidence that the proprietors, managers and patronizing public of hotels, will appreciate the recognition given these deserving men who labor zealously always for the success of the hotel, and the comfort of their patrons.

Certainly, the close relationship of the waiters with those things that are necessary to satisfy the appetite, and their efficient manner in serving the same, should endear the men in the dining room and the head waiter at the door to the heart of every one who enjoys the luxurious comforts of an up-to-date American hotel dining room.

It is true, of course, that to be entitled to such recognition, one should have achieved eminent success in one or more of the high callings of the world. But there is, however, an exception to every rule, and in this case, it is a very justifiable one; for, while it may not be said that these men have achieved success in what is recognized as the higher callings, yet, nevertheless, they have undoubtedly achieved success in that calling which circumstances have forced a number of them, many of whom, had conditions been otherwise, would have attained positions of eminence in any one of the higher callings into which the natural force of the world's current might have carried them, like other men, who have been unhampered in the development of their natural ability, and unrestricted in their movement through the various channels of operation. As human plants, dwarfed by a force, unnatural to the design of the Creator, that they have made commendable success, and have shown natural ability is a fact which is sufficient under the circumstances, to entitle them to this biographic recognition.

It will also be appreciated that though a head waiter's position may not be regarded as one of the highest callings, his functions, however, are very important in the hotel industry. By no means is the position simply what the title designates. There was a time when the duty of the man bearing the title "Head Waiter," was merely what the title signifies, and nothing more; but to-day, that title is a misnomer, as it fails to express the real duties of the position.

Keeping abreast with the other industries, and the increasing wealth and population of the country, the hotel business has developed to an enormous proportion and demands in the position of a head waiter, or more correctly speaking, superintendent of the dining room, ability very much greater than a mere mastery of the art of good waiting. The colossal wealth of the American Czars, Emperors and Kings of finance, and Captains of the various industries, the increase of the leisure class of wealth, together with the general good-living of the average American, demand for their entertainment in the palatial hotels of this continent, an elegance and grandeur that are seldom enjoyed by the crowned heads of Europe. Naturally, therefore, compatible with these regal surroundings, the head waiter who stands at the dining room door as the vice host, receiving the guests, and paying the extra honors to distinguished patrons as they enter, and at the same time surveying the dining room, seeing that everything in this department is moving in regular order, and is in keeping with the high standard of the house, diplomatically pacifying patrons with real or imaginary grievances, and maintaining proper order in the dining room, among a large number of men, who are under his supervision—sometimes to the number of 400, is selected because he possesses all the qualifications that are necessary to fill these various high positions that are combined under the common title "Head waiter."

While in years past the service was mostly filled by men untrained in intellect, but of great natural ability, it is, however, acquiring now a considerable addition of young men whose minds have been trained. This element is increasing more and more every year, for as the schools and colleges send forth their graduates in greater numbers every succeding year, these graduates, finding the avenue of other industries congested to them, are turning their attention, to a great extent, to that calling which offers them the least resistance, and which years ago had been assigned by common consent to their forefathers. There is no questioning the fact that this increase of intelligence in the service will be of great advantage to the proprietors and patrons of the hotels. That this class of young men did not turn their attention in that direction before, is simply because a false conception was held as to the importance of the occupation. At the same time, however, many of their kinsmen who are now in higher callings, were enabled to get there through the channel of the dining room department in which they had served. This fact in itself has brought, and is bringing many young men of education and good moral training into the service; and it is also being recognized by many who might otherwise have wasted their intelligence in the desert places of idleness, that in the Republic of labor, honest toil for one's daily bread in any vocation, is honorable; and that no matter what the occupation may be, the calling is dignified, proportionately to the amount of intelligence required for the execution. Under these circumstances, there is no reason why the dining room department should not receive the highest intelligence available.

The day is fast approaching, therefore, when every first-class hotel in the country will be able, at short notice, to place in the dining room, a crew of colored waiters, who, in intelligence and efficiency, will be equal to those of any other class of waiters. As a certainty, then, the future is not far distant when a large number of those leading hotels that are not now employing colored waiters, will give preference to them. There is no reason why it should not be done now; the patrons in the majority of cases, prefer colored waiters, and for economic reasons in many cases, the change from them ought not to have been made. But, of course, the rapid rise of the hotel industry, within the past decade, which brought into existence the palatial hotels with their concomitant baronial splendor, caried away from their former bearing, many hotel proprietors and managers who were deluded with the idea that colored waiters could not fit in nicely into the royal splendor of the general surroundings, and, therefore, they changed to white waiters with the initiation of the European plan. There is, however, a very strong and general belief that many of these men have realized the fallacy of the idea, and have discovered that the intelligent polished piece of ebony is just the thing needed to give force of contrast to the marble guests, and at the same time properly distinguish the servitor from those he serves, and gives the exquisite and artistic variety of color-blending to the splendor of the surroundings in the dining room.

There is much reason to believe, therefore, that a change back to colored waiters by many of these hotels, will soon take place. Of course it will come gradually, but come it will.

The colored waiters for generations, and, in fact, from the introduction of the hotel business in this country, have served with much efficiency in the dining room, and have helped, through their good service, to raise the business to the standard it is to-day. No correct history of the American hotel business could be written with the negro waiters left out. Many leading houses have been gradually making the change whenever it was most convenient for them to do so, and as the managers become more confident that they can fill their dining room with a high class of colored men at any time, and at short notice, the change will be made as being most compatible with the service.

To meet this situation, therefore, the advance men among the head waiters, the men who are keen in their conception, and who possess master minds, with the ability and courage to grapple with the condition, are putting forth every effort to educate the men up to the highest standard of efficiency required in the service through the agency of the Head, Second and Side Waiters' National Benefit Association. And it is, indeed, gratifying to be able to say that their efforts are succeeding, as there is, to-day, a much better service in the dining room department of those hotels of which members of the organization are in charge, than ever before.

The principal purpose of this organization, outside of caring for the sick and burying its dead, is to establish schools to educate the side waiters and its members in general, up to the highest degree of efficiency in the dining room, and in the culinary department, so that they may be able to meet the highest requirements, and thereby make their services an economic factor in the success of the hotel business, and increase the comforts of the patrons in the dining room. This high purpose is worthy of the greatest praise; and should receive the highest approval and appreciation, and the liberal encouragement of every hotel employer, be he manager or proprietor. For it is in glorious contrast to the coercive methods of other organizations of labor, whose principal purpose is to dictate to employers whom they should hire at high wages, regardless of the capability of the individual to give service, commensurate with the high wages demanded.

The efforts of this organization are bound to bring forth fruit to the material and mutual advantage of the hotel proprietors and the men in the calling, as well as to the patrons of the dining room.

The ever increasing number of educated young men who are now entering the service to meet its higher requirements, bids fair to raise the calling to an even still higher plain of respect than that in which it has been held in past years.

There is every reason to believe that this organization will become a great power for good and a conspicuous factor in the economy of the hotel industry, and there is no doubt but that the time will soon come when the title "Head Waiter" will be changed to some other title more significant of the real duties performed, such as "Superintendent of the Dining Room," as being more in consonance with the varied requirements of this important position, and to differentiate him from those under him.

It is an unquestionable fact that for some time to come a large number of the more intelligent young men of the race will enter this and other similar callings; for while, of course, this has been going on for years, it has only been done promiscuously, and not as a result of intelligent reasoning; but which is now the case. For it is the conclusive opinion that in many cases, it is better for the young man of education to employ it in those callings in which he can become a factor, thus enabling him to receive more adequate compensation, than to seek those channels in which the resistance is much greater, and the compensation for him generally inadequate.   E. A. MACCANNON.

HISTORY

OF THE FOUNDING OF THE HEAD AND SECOND WAITERS' NATIONAL BENEFIT ASSOCIATION.

In writing the history of this organization very much cannot be said at so early a period of its existence, more than to narrate the particulars of its founding and the events occurring since its inception. The time will come, however, it is greatly hoped, when much can be said of the work and great achievements of this association and the men composing it. Many of whom, undoubtedly, are destined to grace the pages of their race's history; some of them, probably, will pass beyond this bound and enter into the great area of their country's and the world's history by reason of some great achievement in one or more of the departments of the world's callings. Process of time will eventually differentiate the individuals and develop the material among them.

On the 20th day of September, 1899, the HEAD AND SECOND WAITERS' NATIONAL BENEFIT ASSOCIATION was founded in the city of Chicago, Ill. For some time prior to its birth, because of changes often made by some of the leading hotels from colored waiters (their old standby) to white, the necessity was felt of an organization that would periodically bring together the men in the calling for the free interchange of ideas on matters pertaining to the advancement of their calling, and that would unite them in a definite plan to raise, to the highest standard of efficiency, the service in the dining room, through a thorough training of the side waiters and the men in general, to meet the requirement of the time; therefore making them a permanent factor in the economic success of the business, and thus leaving no cause, in that particular feature, to operate as an excuse for their non-employment, or change from their service by the leading hotels in the country.

The matter having been talked about by several of the men and freely discussed wherever two or more head waiters happened to be located, it was decided by the movers that the time had fully come to act. Upon this decision a number of the men met in the early part of 1899, formed a general committee with W. Forrest Cozart, as its chairman and John B. Goins secretary, and appointed a sub-committee to ascertain the views of other head waiters relative to forming a permanent organization. The sub-committee, after corresponding with the head waiters throughout the country and receiving favorable replies, met together with the general committee, in the same year, and rendered a report in which it recommended the holding of a convention in the city of Chicago in the month of September of the same year, 1899, to perfect a permanent organization. This report was adopted and the secretary of the general committee was instructed to send out a call for a convention of head and second waiters. Letters were immediately sent out to every head and second waiter, of color, in the United States, inviting him to attend and advising him of the purpose of the convention.

The prime mover in this affair was W. Forrest Cozart. He was ably assisted by John B. Goins. Of these men too much cannot be said in praise for the valuable services given in bringing the matter to a successful issue. From the moment of its conception until they saw the full fruit in the realization of the purpose, these two men labored incessantly with untiring energy and unflagging zeal to lay the foundation of an organization that would be a monument to the intelligence of the men in the calling, and an inspiration to lift them up. Often, night's dark shadows of disappointment threw a gloom of apparent failure on their endeavors, but they faltered not, the dawn of another morning would meet them still undaunted, set with new resolutions to accomplish the task to which they had set themselves. With others, they sacrificed time and money; ceasing not in their effort until, on that fair September day, when, after the sun, in his majestic march across the heavens, had set upon a perfected organization, leaving them accomplishers and, it may be said, conquerors of many obstacles.

On September 20th, 1899, in Bethel Chapel, Dearborn street, Chicago, Ill., the first meeting of the convention was held. On that memorable occasion about one hundred head and second waiters answered the call and were there gathered from all parts of the country. W. Forrest Cozart, acting as temporary chairman, called the meeting to order, and in an able and impressive address outlined the purposes of the convention. At the close of his address he was elected permanent chairman and John B. Goins secretary of the convention. A committee on permanent organization was then appointed, which later recommended that the convention form itself into a permanent association to be known as the HEAD AND SECOND WAITERS' NATIONAL BENEFIT ASSOCIATION, whose aim and object should be to train and educate the negro waiters up to the highest standard of efficiency required in the calling. The report of the committee was received and its recommendation unanimously adopted.

The convention continued in session for three days. After the preliminary work had been finished, a committee on constitution and by-laws was appointed. In the interval, several interesting and instructive papers were read and discussed. Addresses were delivered by J. J. Miles, of the Plankinton House, Milwaukee, on his twenty-five years' experience as a head waiter, and other prominent head waiters.

F. C. Long, E. T. Montgomery, Charles McCard, H. Pittegrew, Geo. T. Ecton, Capt. Adolph Thomas and Benjamin Tomkins were, among others, the most active during the convention in the formation of the association.

On the third day of the convention the committee on constitution and by-laws reported. After its report was received and adopted and all other business before the convention had been transacted, the convention proceeded to elect officers for the association created. The following officers were elected to serve for one year: W. Forrest Cozart, president; E. T. Montgomery, vice-president; John B. Goins, corresponding secretary; W. Alonza Locke, recording secretary, and Charles McCard, treasurer. A vice-pesident was elected for every State represented in the convention. At the close of the election, a place for holding the next meeting was discussed. The city of Pittsburg was finally selected. Having finished all of its business, the convention adjourned to meet in 1900 in the city of Pittsburg, at the call of the president.

On May 28th, 29th and 30th, 1900, the Second Annual Convention of the Association was held in the city of Pittsburg, Pa. The meeting was opened in the Wylie Avenue, A. M. E. Church, by the president, W. Forrest Cozart.

After the singing of a hymn, Divine blessing was asked by the Pastor of the church, followed by the reading of the minutes of the previous convention, which were approved. After the reading of communications, an address on behalf of the city was delivered by Recorder Deild, which was responded to by Mr. W. Alonza Locke, of the Halliday House, Cairo, Ill.

At this convention the death benefit provided for in the Constitution at the first convention was discussed, with the result that the members residing in Washington, D. C., resigned in a body, rather than pay the assessments levied at the death of members.

In the report of the president, it was shown that 24 hours after the death of one of the members $81.50 was paid to his widow, leaving a balance to be paid of $18.50, and also that through the influence of the president, Mr. Cozart, and the organization, many good positions were secured by several of the members.

On the third day of the convention interesting addresses were delivered on the serving of banquets by Messrs. E. C. Holland, H. Pettigrew, C. Johnson, Gray and many others. The meeting was also addressed by Messrs. Joseph T. Thompson and T. Jones, of Harrisburg, Pa., who started life in the hotel calling, but who had managed by reason of economy and shrewd business ability, to save enough money and had entered into more lucrative business for themselves. All other business having been transacted, the members paid in their dues, and the meeting proceeded to the election of officers. Mr. W. Forrest Cozart was again elected president; W. Alonza Locke, vice-president; E. T. Montgomery, recording secretary; John B. Goins, corresponding secretary, and C. McCard, treasurer. The vice-president from the various States were re-appointed, as also the members of the Board of Managers, after which the convention adjourned to meet, subject to the call of the president.

At the evening of the second day of this convention, a banquet was tendered the visiting members, their wives and friends, in the Masonic Hall, Allegheny City. Three hundred persons sat around the table. Some of Pittsburg's leading colored citizens joined with the committee which was composed of H. Pettigrew, Chairman, Thomas Floyd, C. Johnson, J. T. Gilbert, Geo. Williams, C. McCard, and F. L. Jones.

During the second administration of President Cozart, he, finding himself pressed with other business, and not having sufficient time to attend to the work of the Association, resigned. The reign of government was therefore placed into the hands of the vice-president, Mr. W. Alonza Locke.

From September 23rd, to 25th, 1901, the third annual convention assembled in the city of Buffalo, N. Y. The meetings were held in the Vine Street, A. M. E. Church. President Locke, of Cairo, Ill., called the convention to order, after the invocation of Divine blessing by the Rev. E. A. Johnson. Twenty-eight members responded to the roll call; at the conclusion of which Mayor Conrad Deihl, of the city, delivered an address of welcome, which was responded to by W. Forrest Cozart, then of the Gibson House, Buffalo, N. Y., and also by the Hon. James A. Ross, representative of the colored exhibitors in the Pan-American Exposition.

At the close of the addresses the President delivered his annual address, followed by greetings from the vice-president of the State of Pennsylvania, H. Pettigrew, of Pittsburg, Pa.; John B. Goins, corresponding secretary, and Charles H. McCard, treasurer; also Messrs. Thomas H. Frazier, G. A. Burnett, H. F. Still, G. B. Cranford, W. P. Landon, John A. Gloster, John T. Gilbert, and C. Saunders, of St. Paul. After this, the report of the officers was read and approved. A resolution, deploring the tragic death of President Wm. McKinley, was offered by Mr. E. T. Montgomery; the same was was adopted.

At this convention the members from Washington, D. C., who had resigned at the previous convention, returned, and were accepted. A number of head and second waiters joined the organization at this meeting.

The establishment of a school to train waiters, and an employment bureau, and a civil service examination for the admittance of waiters in the service, were freely discussed. E. T. Montgomery pointed out that the change from colored waiters to white, was materially affecting the colored waiters, and that it was necessary to educate the colored waiters in the checking system and other features of the European plan.

On account of the delinquency of many of the members in paying up the death assessments, the clause of the constitution relating to death benefits and assessments was taken from the Constitution. The officers elected were: W. Alonza Locke, president; E. W. Harper, vice-president; E. C. Holland, corresponding secretary, and W. B. Keys, treasurer. The Board of Managers, consisted of E. T. Montgomery, chairman, Frank P. Thompson, A. E. Jenkins, B. H. Thompson, and T. J. Simons. The convention then adjourned to meet at the call of the president.

The fourth annual convention convened in the city of Washington, D. C., October 13th to 16th, 1902; this convention marked the closing of the second administration of President Locke.

The address of welcome was delivered by Mr. R. S. Locke, (now deceased) of the Shoreham Hotel, Washington, D. C., and was responded to by the president, W. Alonza Locke, in which he stated that one of the principal objects of the association was to educate the men in the hotel calling up to the highest standard of efficiency in the service, and in all the other requirements necessary thereto.

The convention was addressed by C. C. Randolph, of New York; H. Pettigrew, of Pittsburg, Pa., and Mr. W. H. Smiley, of West Superior, Wis. The principal feature of the convention, however, was an address delivered by Mr. Frank P. Thompson, of New York.

After the other business of the convention had been transacted, the election of officers was proceeded with. Frank P. Thompson was elected president, being nominated by his predecessor, Mr. W. Alonza Locke; E. W. Harper, was elected vice president; E. C. Holland, recording secretary, and W. B. Keys, treasurer; all of these were re-elected with the single exception of the president. The Board of Directors consisted of E. T. Montgomery, Chairman. T. J. Simons, E. A. Jenkins, B. F. Tompkins and C. M. Farrar, all of whom were also re-elected, with the exception of Mr. Farrar. The convention then adjourned to meet at the call of the president.

At the close of the convention the members were sumptuously entertained by the head waiters of Washington, D. C., and thus ended the business of the Fourth Annual Convention of the Association.

Mr. Thompson, soon after his election, concluded that something ought to be done to infuse new life into the organization, and, after due consideration, decided that certain changes were necessary to its progress. He therefore, consulted with his Board of Managers, who agreed with him, and thereupon the members were communicated with, and an expression of opinion requested. The consensus of opinion being favorable to such changes, at the fifth annual convention, which met at Atlantic City, N. J., on October 13th, 1903, the following changes were put into operation. The name of the Association was changed to be hereafter known as the Head, Second and Side Waiters' National Benefit Association, thereby admitting to membership the side waiters also. A new constitution, making provision for sick and death benefits was also adopted, and a committee appointed in whom was vested the management of the Association during an administration. This convention was largely attended, and much enthusiasm was manifested.

After the president had delivered his annual address, the convention was addressed by Recorder Babcock, of Atlantic City, who extended a welcome to the delegates. Also, during the sessions, by W. Forrest Cozart, R. L. Lipscomb, R. F. Trusty, the Rev. Dr. Cook, Andrew I. Woodlyn, who responded to the address of welcome made by Recorder Babcock, the Rev. Dr. Jolly, Dr. Morris, W. Walls, E. C. Holland, Charles Ferguson, George Robb, Wm. J. Fisher, Rev. Dr. Deaver, W. T. Jones, Morris K. Holland, G. A. Burnett, the Rev. Dr. Townsend, W. A. Fisher, and E. A. Maccannon, of the Gwendolyn Publishing Co., (successor to the New Era Publishing Co.) of N. Y., thus closing the first period of the Thompson administration. All other business having been transacted on the fourth day of the convention, they then proceeded to the election of officers, which resulted in the re-election of the following: Frank P. Thompson, president; W. E. Harper, vice-president; E. C. Holland, secretary; Mr. C. M. Farrar was elected treasurer in place of Mr. W. B. Keys. The Committee of Arrangements was composed of Frank P. Thompson, C. C. Randolph and Fred Allen, of New York City; A. I. Woodlyn, Philadelphia, Pa.; J. M. Butler, Atlantic City, N. J.; after which the convention adjourned. The members were entertained by some of the leading head waiters of the city. A number of new members were added to the roll of membership at this meeting.

It is now reported that since the change in the organization, the membership has more than doubled itself, and the organization is fast becoming one of the strongest and most influential of the race in America.

Owing to the recent fire in Baltimore, the last convention was held in Atlantic City, N. J., on June 6th, 1904, instead of at Baltimore.

FRANK P. THOMPSON.

President Head, Second and Side Waiters' National Benefit Association.

Headwaiter, Hotels Champlain, Bluff Point, Clinton Co., N. Y. and Ponce de Leon, St. Augustine, Fla.

FRANK P. THOMPSON,

PRESIDENT OF THE HEAD, SECOND AND SIDE WAITERS' NATIONAL BENEFIT ASSOCIATION.

The subject of this sketch, Mr. Frank P. Thompson, was born in the city of Charlestown, Jefferson County, Va., on the 24th day of July, 1855. He received his education at Carlisle, Pa., to which place his parents had moved in his early age.

In 1871, he entered the hotel service. His first engagement was at the Ocean House, Cape May, N. J. After seven years of service at different houses, during which time he went through the various grades of his calling, he was promoted to the position of a head waiter, which position he has since held, serving with the highest efficiency in some of the leading hotels in the United States.

Mr. Thompson is a man of portly appearance, with a gentlemanly carriage, and in manners, is polite and agreeable; possesses considerable intellectual culture. He is gifted with the essential qualification of his calling, viz.: the faculty to grasp quickly the peculiarities of the patrons of his hotel and to dispose of difficult questions in a way to satisfy even the most exacting. Though not demonstrative, he is, naturally, a man of very strong individuality, and is looked upon by his brethren in the calling as the "Dean of the Commanders of the Dining Room," if not in length of service, in the respect in which he is held by all classes of men, and the reputation he has established for himself among the hotel proprietors and managers throughout the country.

As a commander, he has the loyal support and respect of every one under him; and though a strict disciplinarian, he is a very kind-hearted man and treats his men with much consideration. He is one of the most proficient head waiters in the country, believing in nothing less than the highest efficiency in the performance of one's duty. Being a man of exemplary character, he is quick to move from among the men in his employ those who are inclined to deviate from the rules of good morals, maintaining that their baneful influence not only demoralizes the others but injuriously affects the standing of all others of the race engaged in the calling. It is his belief that the fault sometimes among head waiters in not weeding out the bad from the good, is one of the causes of the change made in many hotels from colored to white waiters.

Mr. Thompson is a careful observer of current events and is particularly interested in everything that concerns his race. He is an optimist on what the future has in store for his race, and is always ready to help with his time and purse any enterprise undertaken for its benefit. He is also a stockholder in four or five enterprises conducted by members of his race.

One thing particularly in which Mr. Thompson takes great pride is the fact that he has not an enemy in the world. If he has, he says he does not know of any reason for same, as he does not remember ever meeting any one in a social or business way that he cannot meet again with the same feeling of good will that marked their first acquaintance.

Up to this present time, Mr. Thompson has served as head waiter for twenty-eight seasons at two of the principal summer and winter hotels in the country, viz.: fifteen consecutive seasons in command of the dining room of the "Hotel Ponce de Leon," St. Augustine, Fla., and thirteen consecutive seasons at the " Hotel Champlain," Bluff Point, Clinton County, N. Y. Among the others he has served during his career as a head waiter are: the "Carleton," Jacksonville, Fla.; the "Continental," Narragansett Pier, R. I.; "St Augustine Hotel," St. Augustine, Fla.; the "Manhansett," Shelter Island, Suffolk County, L. I.; the "Howland House," Long Branch, N. J.; "Magnolia Spring Hotel," Magnolia, Clay County, Fla.; "Indian Harbor Hotel," Greenwich, Conn.; "San Marco," St. Augustine, Fla.; "Kaaterskill," Catskill Mountains, N. Y.; the "Vendome," Boston, Mass., and "Fort Williams Hotel," Lake George, N. Y.

Mr. Thompson was elected a member of the board of directors of the HEAD AND SECOND WAITERS' NATIONAL BENEFIT ASSOCIATION, at the annual convention held in Buffalo, N. Y., September, 1901; unanimously elected president of the association at the convention held in Washington, D. C., October, 1902, and re-elected in the convention held at Atlantic City, N. J., October, 1903.

He is one of the most progressive members and has great hopes in the future of this organization, the object of which is not only beneficial but for the purpose of raising the standard of efficiency in the service among the colored waiters. After careful study of the situation, Mr. Thompson has reached the conclusion that the colored head and side waiters can only maintain their hold on the leading hotels by the exhibition of the highest efficiency and the ability to render service as good or better than any other race in the calling. It is safe to believe that the conclusion of Mr. Thompson is correct. As a leader he is conservative and is a close student of affairs, drawing his conclusions not from sentiment, but from the logic that follows a careful analytical investigation of conditions.

At the age of forty-nine, Mr. Thompson is in the prime of health and bids fair some day to utilize his capacity for business in some other calling that will add greater prestige in the industrial world to the branch of the human family with which he is identified.

W. ALONZA LOCKE,

Headwaiter, The Halliday Hotel, Cairo, Ill., and Ex-Pres. Head, Second and Side Waiters' National Benefit Association.

W. ALONZA LOCKE.

The subject of this sketch, Mr. W. Alonza Locke, was born on March 28th, 1874, at Rutherford in the State of Tennessee, where his early days were spent, and where he engaged in various kinds of employment while attending school. His parents died when he was but a lad, and from the age of eleven he was under the care of a grandmother.

At the early age of fifteen Mr. Locke entered the hotel business and was employed as general errand boy at what was then known as the Corley House. As he became more and more acquainted with the various duties, he was allowed to assist in waiting during the meal hours, an opportunity which he gladly embraced, and the duties of which he performed with much pleasure. As a result of his careful attention to duty, he was finally permitted to give his entire attention to this work.

Mr. Locke attended school about six months of the year, but his education is principally due to the fact that he continued his studies at home up until he was eighteen years of age. After this he went to Cairo, Ill., and there secured a job as dish carrier in the Halliday House. After serving in this capacity for three weeks, he was promoted to the rank of a waiter; this position he held for a period of two years, at the expiration of which time he was given a Captaincy. One year after this he secured a position in Springfield, Ill., at the Leland Hotel, which was, at that time, the leading hotel in that city. This, however, he held for a short period only, having obtained a position as a porter on a railroad. Not very long after this, Mr. Locke was offered the position of head waiter of the Halliday House by his former employer, Mr. L. P. Parker, and on the 19th of August, 1895, he took up his position as such. He continued in this capacity for several years, notwithstanding the very many offers that were made him to change.

At the completion of the Hotel Gayoso, Mr. Locke was engaged as one of the head waiters, but as the house was run exclusively on the European plan he thought it wise to accept the position of second waiter, which he did, and remained in this service until June 1st, 1902, when he was sent back in charge of the Halliday House, and where he still remains.

Although Mr. Locke has been engaged in the hotel business during all these years, he has never discontinued his studies, and a few years ago entered an academy, where he spent two years, while still continuing in his business.

At the first convention of the Head and Second Waiters' National Benefit Association, held in Chicago, in 1899, Mr. Locke was elected recording secretary; vice-president at the convention held in Pittsburg, Pa., in 1900, and upon the resignation of Mr. W. Forrest Cozart, succeeded to the presidency. At the convention held in Buffalo, N. Y., on September 25th, 1901, he was regularly elected president.

Mr. Locke is a great lover of literature, a conservative business man and a deep thinker; and though but a young man, he gives evidence of a bright future and a successful career. It is said of him that he is ever zealous in the cause of his race, and untiring in his efforts to inculcate in those under him such principles as make for a higher elevation and a better recognition of those in his calling.

EDWARD W. HARPER.

At Nassau, N. P., Bahama Islands, on September 5th, 1853, Edward W. Harper was born. He came at an early age to America, settling down in Philadelphia. At the age of fourteen, having received a fairly good education in the public schools, he went to sea as a cabin boy on a merchant ship, sailing into foreign ports. He remained on this vessel one year. Returning to Philadelphia, he got a job to drive a carriage, and at this he worked another year. Becoming tired, he left, and in succession, tried dentistry, farming, horse-trading, team-driving and waiting in various hotels for five years.

At the expiration of this time, having saved up a little money, he opened a first-class restaurant in Philadelphia. Failing to achieve desired success, he closed up this business, and finally determined to make waiting his chosen calling. He thenceforth went from mountain to seaside resorts, city hotels, restaurants and private parties, every year increasing his knowledge in the service. He continued in this manner until the year 1875, when Mr. W. R. Shipley, one of the leading head waiters in his day, promoted him to first assistant head waiter in the famous Congress Hall Hotel, at Atlantic City, N. J. Mr. Shipley assured Mr. Harper that he possessed the ability to master the service in all of its branches, and further said to him: "My boy! if you stick to me, I will make you as popular as is Pop Shipley." Mr. Harper remained with him until his death, which was a sad loss to Mr. Harper.

In 1876, the year of the Centennial, Mr. Harper had then grown more confident of his ability. He served during that great celebration in the dining rooms of the Continental and the Girard Hotels, and also for Mr. Leland on the Centennial grounds. Leaving this latter place he went with Mr. John Tracey, who was then steward on the steamship *Junetta,* plying between Philadelphia, New Orleans, and Havana, Cuba. Mr. Tracey afterwards left the ship and leased the Green's Hotel, at which place Mr. Harper remained with him for several months. Finding Philadelphia somewhat dull, he left and went to Boston, thence to Providence. While at this place, Mr. Frank P. Thompson engaged him as second waiter at the Continental Hotel, Narragansett Pier. At the close of the season he returned to Providence, and became head parlor man at the new Narra-

E. W. HARPER,

Headwaiter, Cataract Hotel, Niagara Falls, N. Y.; Ex-Vice-President Head, Second and Side Waiters' National Benefit Association.

gansett Hotel. While there, he declined Mr. Thompson's offer to go South during the winter months, but the following summer returned with him to the Continental. At the close of this season, Mr. Harper went to the Benedict House, Pawtucket, R. I., as head waiter, where he remained until January, 1879. From this place he went to the Carlton House, Jacksonville, Fla., with Mr. Thompson, and at the end of that season to Charleston, S. C., from whence he went to again join Mr. Thompson for the summer at the famous Manhasset House, Shelter Island, N. Y. While at this place he engaged with a wealthy family of Providence, with whom he remained until the summer of 1880, when he again went with Mr. Thompson to the Manhasset House, as first assistant.

Mr. Harper was next found at the old Pulaski House, Savannah, Ga., as second head waiter. At the end of five weeks, however, he was offered the position of head waiter, which he at first declined; but being urged upon, he finally accepted, and assumed the command in that capacity, receiving at the close of the season a first-class reference from the manager, and a record of having given to the house the most successful season it had ever had.

May, 1881, found him again in Philadelphia at the Continental Hotel, joining Mr. Thompson again in the winter at the St. Augustine Hotel, Fla. While there, he was offered the position as head waiter at the Scriven House, Savannah, Ga., at his own price, which he accepted. At the close of the season, he went from there to the Columbia Hotel, Lebanon Springs, N. Y., and in 1882 to the Larkin House, Palatka, Fla. On account, however, of an epidemic of smallpox, the house was closed. Mr. Harper, after this, went to the Hotel Warwick, Newport News, as head waiter on a contract for three months, but remained for a period of three years. During this time he became popularly known to hotel proprietors thoughout the country, as one of the most progressive and successful dining room superintendents, and his services were everywhere sought after by hotel proprietors. Accepting an offer, he secured leave of absence, and went to the Clarendon Hotel, Saratoga Springs, for the summer, and returned to his charge at the Warwick at the close of the season. From there he went to the Larkin House, Watch Hill, R. I., and then to the Brunswick, Boston; resigning from there to go back to the Larkin in the summer of '87. At the close of this season, he took to railroading; and finally, in 1888, returned to the Larkin for the third season. In the fall, Mr. Warren Leland engaged him for the new Leland, at Syracuse, N. Y. At this place he remained two years, until the hotel was burned down. After this he went back to railroading until the spring of 1891, when he went to the Rockingham, Narragansett Pier. At the close of the season he went South and opened the Oglethorpe, Brunswick, Ga., and returned to the Rockingham in the spring of 1892. While there, he was engaged to take charge of the Tift House, Buffalo, until time to open the Rockingham, from which he was called to the Chicago Beach Hotel, during the great rush at the World's Fair. He next went to the Oglethorpe, and from there to the Prospect House, and thence to the Tift House. In brief, we may say that Mr. Harper has been in charge of the dining rooms of twelve of the most aristocratic hotels in the United States, since the year 1895. Many of which he had before served for several seasons. Among those not already mentioned, are the Cataract House, Niagara Falls, N. Y., of which he is still in charge; the Royal Poinciana, Palm Beach, Fla., under Mr. Chas. Booker; the United States Hotel, Boston, under Mr. O. M. Jasper; the Mansion House, Brooklyn, N. Y., of which he has been in charge until very recently.

An evidence of Mr. Harper's sterling qualities and progressive ability is the fact that he has been re-employed again and again by such hotel proprietors as Mr. M. D. F. Larkin, Mr. Warren Leland, Mr. Frank M. Rogers, and Mr. J. B. Burns, of the Rockingham, who on one occasion called on Mr. Harper and said "Harper, my dining room has never been conducted in the efficient manner, and with the success as when you were in charge. We want you to come back to us at your own price of compensation, and remain with us as long as we run that hotel." To this request, Mr. Harper complied, and remained with him during his proprietorship.

Mr. Harper is the vice-president of the Head, Second and Side Waiters' National Benefit Association, enjoying the honor of several re-elections. He was among the very first one sought out by those who conceived the idea of perfecting an organization, viz.: Messrs. Cozart, Goins and Montgomery, as they felt that a man with Mr. Harper's reputation in the hotel service, was necessary to add to the prestige of the organization.

Thus it is, that the cabin boy, who at so early an age, left his home and kindred, to come to a foreign country, finding himself in a strange land; a land of peculiar and complex atmosphere; the boy who at the age of fourteen, had acquired a sufficient education in the face of, and under such conditions as were baneful to the growth of his manhood, and who by his varied experience thus gained has, at the meridian of his life, established a reputation for intelligence, fidelity and sagacity as a dining room superintendent, that is equalled by few, and excelled by none in his calling.

One of the elements which adds materially to Mr. Harper's success is the fact that he is very methodical in his business. No detail is too small to pass unnoticed in the performance of his duty. He employs, as a rule, only the highest intelligence that can be secured for the service.

E. C. HOLLAND,

Headwaiter, Clarendon Hotel,
Ex-Secretary, H., S. and S. W. N. B. Assn.

E. C. HOLLAND.

E. C. Holland was born on April 29th, 1865, in the quiet little town of Rockymount, Va. His father was one of those substantial farmers, whose thriftiness has enabled them to be the principal landowners in several of the counties of the State, and it was in this healthy occupation that young Holland was employed until he reached the age of seventeen years. In 1882, he felt that he would like to try some other occupation, and secured employment at the Cabell House, in his native town. In this house there was not much waiting, all that was required of him was to get all the food from the kitchen that had been cooked at each meal, and after placing it on the table, the guests would come in and help themselves. As perfunctory as were these duties, the lessons that Mr. Holland learned during his six months at this house were useful to him, for they tended to dispel the greenness of the farm hand and to give him that confidence which can only be gained by coming in contact with the business men of the country. To a man of Mr. Holland's ambitious disposition, the information he gained from the conversation of the guests at the Cabell House, acted as a stimulus to his desire to go somewhere else where the opportunities for advancement in the occupation he had chosen for a living, were better than in his native town.

In 1883 he, therefore, left his home and went to Roanoke, Va., and secured employment in the new and magnificent Hotel Roanoke. His aptness and strict attention to his duties soon qualified him as a proficient waiter.

In November, 1884, he left Roanoke and journeyed to Richmond, where he remained for a short time in the employ of Ford's Hotel. Leaving Richmond, he went to Baltimore and worked at the Eutaw House. From Baltimore he went to Boston, where he soon found employment at Young's Hotel, and in March of 1886, he went over to the Vendome in the same city. The year 1887 found Mr. Holland in Cincinnati, Ohio, where he worked at the Burnett House, and in the fall of the same year, at the Arcade Hotel, Springfield, Ohio. With the promise of advancement he went to the Monongahela House, Pittsburg, Pa., and was soon promoted to third waiter and later to second head waiter. In May, 1889, he resigned from the Monongahela House, and was engaged as one of the crew that went to Duluth, Minn., to open the new Spalding Hotel. At this hotel he became second waiter and subsequently head waiter. Leaving Duluth in 1891, he went to Chicago, Ill., to the Auditorium Hotel. Since then Mr. Holland has filled the following positions: For four seasons he was head waiter at Kay's Park Hotel, Lake Geneva, Wis.; one year head waiter at the Lake Shore Hotel, Chicago; one year private waiter at the Hotel Cadillac, Detroit, Mich.; from January, 1898 to May, 1900, head waiter of the Hotel Ruffner, Charleston, W. Va., and second waiter from May, 1900 to September of the same year at the Hotel Chittenden, Columbus, Ohio, from which place he went to the Hotel Clarendon, Zanesville, Ohio, as head waiter, a position he has held up to the present time.

It may be mentioned, also, that the season of 1896, Mr. Holland spent on the Lakes, as head waiter of the palatial steel steamship *Manitou,* belonging to the L. M. & L. S. T. Co. Everyone who has traveled on the great lakes, knows the magnificent steamer *Manitou,* for it is a steamer which is not surpassed in excellence by any of the ocean greyhounds.

Mr. Holland was the genial and efficient secretary of the Head, Second and Side Waiters' National Benefit Association, up to December of 1903. He was elected at the convention held in Buffalo, N. Y., September, 1901, re-elected at the convention held in Washington, D. C., October, 1902, and again re-elected at the convention held in Atlantic City, N. J., October, 1903; but owing to the stress of other important business, Mr. Holland resigned the office as above mentioned. He conducted his office in a very businesslike manner, displaying much ability and deserves much credit and praise for the valuable services he has rendered the organization.

THOMAS J. SIMONS.

The road to success, while winding, leads ever onward and upward, and a steady march and a determined effort are two of the requisite elements to reach it. It was with the knowledge of these facts in mind that the subject of this sketch—one of the most popular and accomplished head waiters in the country—Mr. Thomas J. Simons, started on his career to make a living.

Mr. Simons was born in the famous old State of South Carolina, in the town of Columbia, on the 25th of May, 1860.

He received a fair common school education, and put in his first three years of service as a valet to the distinguished statesman, the Hon. J. H. McDuffey. While in this occupation he determined to enter the hotel service, and in the year 1876, accepted an engagement as a side waiter in the Charleston Hotel, Charleston, S. C., under the head waitership of Mr. Edward Chatham.

The training which Mr. Simons received while serving under Mr. Chatham, was so thorough that, after three successive seasons as side waiter at the Grand Union Hotel, Saratoga Springs, he was advanced to the head waitership of that house.

Though still a young man, he made himself so efficient that he soon became one of the most popular and best known head waiters throughout the country.

In the year 1880 he became head waiter in the dining room of the Eagle Hotel, an aristocratic resort in Asheville, N. C. At this house Mr. Simons' reputation as a commander of the dining room was increased by the exceptional service which he rendered.

He has served with much credit the following hotels: The Haywood, the White Sulphur Spring Hotel, Waynesville, N. C., which latter place he remained for two years; also the Charlotte House of said city, where he likewise served two years.

In 1887 Mr. Simons took charge of the dining room of the Lakeview, at Birmingham, Ala., and in the following year accepted the charge at the Exchange Hotel, at Montgomery, Ala., going from this place to the Anderson House, at Lexington, Ala.

The year 1890 found him in charge of the dining room of the Armstrong House, Rome, Ga., returning from there to Birmingham to take charge of the Caldwell Hotel in 1891.

T. J. SIMONS,

Headwaiter, White Stone Lithia Springs Hotel, White Stone Springs, S. C.

In the spring of the following year, Mr. Simons was head waiter of the Belmont House, Asheville, N. C. About this time he became so well-known that he was employed during the World's Fair to direct the affairs in the dining room of that exclusive resort in Chicago known as the Columbus Club.

In 1894 he took charge of the noted Rockingham Hotel dining room, at Narragansett Pier, R. I., and in the following year became head waiter of the Atlantic Hotel, Morehead City, N. C.

From the fall of 1895 to 1897 he had charge of the Sweetwater Park Hotel, Lithia Springs, Ga., and in 1898, during the Spanish-American War, Mr. Simons was in command of the dining room in the Lookout Mountain Inn, on the battle-scarred mountain of Tennessee.

During the winter of 1899 he was head waiter of the Plaza Hotel, Rockledge, Fla., and the next summer found him in charge of the Tates Spring Hotel, Tenn.

The following year he served as head waiter at the Duval Hotel, Jacksonville, Fla. In the summer of that year, he took charge of the dining room of the Jackson Hotel, Atlantic City, N. J.

In the fall of 1901 Mr. Simons was called to command the dining room of the Endicott Hotel, New York City; remaining there until the spring of 1902, when he went to the Victoria Hotel, at Larchmont, N. Y.

Mr. Simons has spent the greater part of his life in hotel work, and he now enjoys the friendship of thousands, both among his race, as well as the Anglo-Saxon.

He is a member of the Head, Second and Side Waiters' National Benefit Association, and one of the Board of Directors. He is also chairman of the Board of Directors of the Atlantic City Head Waiters' Benefit Association, and has the honor of being a member of the National Hotel Keepers' Protective Association. Mr. Simons is also a high degree Mason, and a member of the Grand United Order of Odd Fellows.

In the year 1887 Mr. Simons was united in marriage with Miss Mary C. Calloway, and his family now consists of two sons and one daughter, all of whom we trust will portray the noble traits of character found in Mr. Simons. He owns a beautiful residence on Hill street, Asheville, N. C., where his family now resides.

ROBERT H. GRANT.
Headwaiter McLure House, Wheeling, W. Va.

ROBERT H. GRANT.

In the State of Virginia, from which so many presidents have come, and which has given birth to a large number of successful men in other walks of life, Robert H. Grant was born, in the town of Warrenton and county of Fauquier, in the year 1846. In climbing the ladder to success, young Grant's pathway and early life were, naturally different to those of the other great men Virginia has produced. Had it not been so, we might now be heralding the success of a great statesman, professional man or a captain of some large industry, instead of that of one in a minor, though honorable calling of a HEAD WAITER. However this may be, success is success in any calling; and he who reaches the top of the ladder in his calling, as a rule, demonstrates superior ability, and, therefore, is as worthy of notice, though his may be the humble, as he whose calling the world recognizes as being of the lofty; for it is true in every calling: "Many are called but few are chosen."

Starting as a bell-boy, Mr. Grant commenced his hotel career in the old Warren-Green Hotel in his native town. In 1863, at the age of seventeen he left his native hearth for Parkersburg, Va., where he remained until the year 1876. While in this place, he served in the old Spencer House as a side waiter, for two years; after which, like most young men, in a migratory state of mind, he went to the Swan House in the same city. Remaining in the city of Parkersburg for thirteen years, he felt at the end of this period a desire to see other places, and putting the desire into action, he moved on February 1, 1876, to Wheeling, W. Va., and immediately after secured a place in the Warren McLure House, where he remained for but two and one-half months as a side waiter, during which time he demonstrated those qualities in a side waiter that make the successful head waiter. Feeling confident that he had mastered the art in his chosen calling, and that he had reached the meridian of efficiency and therefore was capable of assuming the responsibilities of a higher position in this calling, he gave up his place as a side waiter and left the hotel. Five days after he left (May 23rd), the management sent for him and gave him full charge of the dining room as a head waiter; and here at this period he entered the zone of the position of a commander, and thus commenced a worthy and successful career as dining room superintendent.

In the year 1879 he went with Mr. Warner to the Stevenson House at St. Catherine, Canada, where he remained for two seasons, '79-'80. Returning to Wheeling, W. Va., he again took charge of the dining room of the McLure House, at which place he remained until the spring of 1886.

The migratory spirit again took hold of the young man, and with the ambition of "more worlds to conquer," he resigned his position and went with the Swartz Bros. to Zanesville, Ohio, where he superintended the dining room of the Clarendon Hotel for eighteen months. Giving up this position, he once more returned to the McLure House, Wheeling, W. Va., and there held that place until January of the year 1891. At this period his reputation as a successful dining room manager became widely known, and receiving many calls to different places, he accepted, for a change, the call to the Windsor Hotel, where he remained until June of the year 1894, when he was again requested to take charge of the McLure House. Having proved himself to be a man of intrinsic value and much ability in the management of the dining room, his resignation was received but accepted with much reluctancy by the management of the Windsor. Thus, Mr. Grant returned to the McLure, the place of his first charge as a head waiter, older in age and with the progressiveness of a mature and active student in the affairs of his calling, and has brought up the service in the dining room of this hotel to a high state of efficiency and to a position second to none in the country.

Though away several times from the McLure to other hotels he has, nevertheless, through the many changes of proprietors, served every owner that has managed this hotel from 1876 to the present time, and with much satisfaction to every one and credit to himself.

Mr. Grant displays considerable administrative and diplomatic ability in the performance of his duty.

Simple as the position of HEAD WAITER, or more correctly speaking, SUPERINTENDENT of the dining room, of an up-to-date hotel appears to be, few have any idea of the keen executive, diplomatic and general ability necessary to maintain a well ordered dining room, and to continually keep it up to the standard in consonance with the state of elegance and grandeur which the increasing fabulous wealth of the Americans demands in their hotel accommodations. That, for a man, to be taken from the side, placed in full charge and continue in charge of the same hotel for nearly thirty years, throughout various changes of management, and to be recalled whenever he leaves, speaks volumes for his capability, soberness and integrity.

Mr. Grant is an active member of the HEAD, SECOND AND SIDE WAITERS' NATIONAL BENEFIT ASSOCIATION; and he believes firmly that the calling of a waiter can be raised to a higher plane through a better standard of intelligence and a more manly and moral tone in the side waiters and the superintendents generally, the concomitant of which will be a greater demand for the services of the men.

Such men as Mr. Grant, a strict disciplinarian, yet with an abundance of human sympathy, and much consideration for those under him, a conscientious and precise performer of his duties, will be leaders in any calling, given the equal chances of others in the world's field of operation.

THOMAS A. MORRIS,
Headwaiter, Battery Park Hotel, Asheville, N. C.

THOMAS A. MORRIS.

Thomas A. Morris was born forty-five years ago in the little town of Sugarhill, McDowell County, N. C. His parents were very poor and humble. They were deprived of those natural opportunities which are the birthright of all men, by the deplorable institution of slavery. It was therefore impossible for them to give the necessary training to their son, which is the desire of all God-fearing parents to do. The consequence of this was that young Morris had to shift for himself and "just grow up," acquiring as best he could an education. His first training in the calling was in that quaint old-fashioned tavern or hotel, Mountain Hotel, in Morganton, N. C. At that time the old time "top and march system" was in use and the bill of fare was given to the waiter orally by the head cook (the word "chef" was not in use then), nor was there any regulation costume, any costume was good enough, and being attired in whatever one possessed or was nearest to hand, a waiter was ready for work, provided he was neat and clean.

Though this beginning was crude, it was in this humble capacity that Mr. Morris laid the foundation for the important and responsible positions which he has since filled. It was at this small hotel that he mapped out his career, and, as he early decided to pursue this line of work for a living, determined to succeed by making himself and his services always valuable to his employers. Judging his success from his present position this plan of action can well be taken as an example by many of the young men of to-day who are failures because they seem to think that their employers ought to look out for their interests when they do not look out for the interests of their employers. To quote Mr. Morris' words on this subject, he says: "My first impressions of my relation to my employer were that my time and services were his during the entire time I was on duty; and my principal policy during my career in the hotel work has been to receive and obey orders, carrying them into execution to the best of my ability, regardless from whom they came. And right here let me say, one of the fundamental principles of success as a waiter, side, second or head, is the ability to give, receive and execute an order promptly with little or no friction."

From the Mountain Hotel he went to the Glenn Apple Springs Hotel, in Burk County, where he remained for many months. From the Springs he went to Asheville, as there was no opening for him in any hotel, rather than remaining idle, he engaged in any work that came to hand. Soon, however, he found an opening at one of the smaller hotels (the Eagle) and from there he went to the Swannano.

When the Battery Park Hotel opened in 1886, Mr. Morris became one of the staff and has remained to the present time at this exclusive hostelry, advancing step by step to the superintendency of the dining room.

From the crude old-time hotel in Morganton, to the Battery Park Hotel, is indeed, a step, but the ability of the man, the efficient service which he rendered, his steadfastness to duty, together with his polite manner were naturally bound to attract attention and bring their merited reward.

It was fortunate for Mr. Morris that when he went to the Battery Park Hotel, he was brought under the influence of that renowned head waiter, John Glascow, now deceased. The memory of this man will be cherished by scores of men besides Mr. Morris, because of his fatherly kindness and his interest in inspiring them in the beginning of their career, which inspiration has led them along the road to success and happiness.

For one season of four months, Mr. Morris was head waiter at Middlesborough, Ky. This was his first experience in an official capacity and having given every satisfaction, he received the commendations of the proprietors and returned to the Battery Park as second man to Mr. Glascow. Since then he has been advanced to the head waitership and has remained as such ever since.

In the years and generations to come such a worthy progress as we chronicle above, might seem insignificant when compared to the heights of successive achievements to which the progenies of his kindred shall have ascended; but then the natural acorn of ability which is found in such men as Mr. Morris and many others in various other callings, will have a more fertile field and a freer atmosphere in which to grow and develop into the world's giant oak, than that in which it was Mr. Morris' fortune to operate and breathe.

C. C. RANDOLPH.

C. C. Randolph was born at Charlotte Court House, Va. His childhood days were uneventfully passed among the beautiful sceneries of the now famous and historical place of his nativity, but, like many others of his kindred, at that peculiar period of the world's dark history, under the humid pressure of an adverse and humiliating social condition.

As a youth, young Randolph was always leading in whatever he undertook to do, be it work or play. He endeavored to do things with a thoroughness which exemplified a genius born to succeed. As he advanced in age, the same characteristic advanced with him, and thus in his mature years this capacity has developed to the extent of giving him the mastery over the intricate art of his calling, and makes him to-day one of the leading superintendents of hotel dining room—a position better known in the United States as HEAD WAITER.

After the shameful pages of his country's history were washed and redeemed with the crimson blood of a nation's army, mingled amongst which were two hundred thousand of the valiant sons of his kindred, and the powdered smoke of battle, in that trying period and sanguinary event which gave historical fame to Appomattox and Charlotte Court House, had been cleared, and the sunlight of freedom had shone upon his head, and he had breathed the ozone of liberty into his depressed lungs, he started out to help himself in life, with an ambition to reach the highest plane to which his natural ability could, and the force of circumstances would raise him. His first employment was with a doctor with whom he remained five years. Leaving him, he took service with a Mr. Cox, at Dutch Gap, on the James River, where he remained ten years, serving as driver, butler, and general utility man. While at this occupation he became attracted to the vocation of waiting, on seeing, when he visited the city of Richmond, on several occasions, the waiters there in their white jacket and other bright and neat uniforms: he, therefore, gave up his place with Mr. Cox, and went to Richmond, where he immediately secured employment in the Exchange Hotel, and thus commenced his career in the calling of a waiter.

In course of time he went from the Exchange to the Ballard; then to the Spotwood, and thence to the St. Charles Hotel. After going

C. C. RANDOLPH.

Member of Managing Committee, Head, Second and Side Waiters' National Benefit Association.

Headwaiter Sherman Square Hotel, New York City and Hotel Edgemere, Edgemere, L. I.

the rounds of the Richmond hotels, his ambition craved for a place which offered greater opportunities to success. As the metropolis of a country is most always the center of attraction to which genius and ambition are generally drawn, naturally young Randolph turned his attention to the North and was attracted to New York, for which place he set out. The North, then, as in earlier days, and even now, was the light of day to which many of his kinsmen, when in their night of darkness, flew.

It was on a Wednesday morning, bright and early, in the month when the song birds return to the North from their Southern wintry flight, and all nature is aglow with life, that young Randolph, in his gravitation directly from Richmond, set his feet in the city of New York. The sun shone that morning with an illumination of joy, and its rays kissed the verdant earth, sending streams of gladness everywhere, changing the chilly atmosphere which loiters behind from wintry sombre days, as if to remind one of the proximity of the season just passed. So beautiful and grand was the opening of the morning of his arrival that it appeared as if the God of the sky, the creator of Heaven and Earth, had specially willed it as a glad welcome to a purer atmosphere than that from which he came.

Soon after his arrival in New York he obtained work on a river steamboat running between New York and Providence, on which he stayed for six months. At the end of this period he met old man Pully, of the old Metropolitan, New York City, from which many a head waiter has graduated, and who took an interest in him and, without any solicitation on the part of the young man, engaged him for the Metropolitan. There he remained until the hotel gave way to the imperial march of commerce. He then went to the Jones House, where he remained for three years, going to different watering places in the summer months and returning in the winter. During this period he was captain of the watch in some of the leading and largest hotels which he served.

After serving his term on the side for several years, his integrity as a man, ability as a waiter, and proficiency in the art of his calling being recognized, he was promoted to the position of second waiter, in which capacity he served with much credit in many of the leading houses in the States.

At last Mr. Randolph reached the goal of his ambition, the place to which every intelligent and ambitious side waiter aspires, if he intends to make waiting a life calling. His first start as a dining room superintendent was at the Hotel St. Stephen, Eleventh street and Broadway, New York City.

In 1888 he took down a crew of colored waiters to Florida, whose expenses down were the first to be paid by the hotel, to open the Cordoza House, at St. Augustine. It was so arranged that the management paid the traveling expenses of the men, furnished them with sleeping berths down, boarded them at the expense of the house, and commenced their pay from the day they left New York, a condition which never existed before until it was insisted on by Mr. Randolph, who, on being offered the position to take charge and open the house, made it a condition precedent to his accepting. So desirous was the management to secure his valuable service that it readily acquiesced to his proposition; and thus was established an advantageous precedent for the men in the calling. He retained charge of this house for five consecutive winter seasons, until the year 1892, when he took charge of and opened the Sherman Square Hotel, New York City, where he still remains. This is the only first class hotel in New York City that has retained colored waiters continuously from the day of its opening; it, therefore, speaks well of Mr. Randolph's ability and the efficiency of colored waiters, when carefully selected.

While at the Sherman Square, for these many years, Mr. Randolph has utilized his summer vacation presiding over the dining rooms of the following hotels: Masconoma, Manchester-by-the-Sea, Mass., for five seasons; Champlain, Lake Champlain, N. Y., one season; Braslin, Lake Hopatcong, N. J., two seasons; Victoria, Larchmont, N. Y., two seasons, and Hotel Edgemere, Edgemere, L. I., of which he was the first to open and of which place he is now again in charge.

Mr. Randolph is a very intelligent man, and possesses a considerable amount of native shrewdness and practical business ability. He is conversant with human nature, being a close student thereof, and is the embodiment of systematic management in his affairs. This may be better understood when it is known that from the position where he stands during the meal hours he receives with grace the patrons of the house, and at the same time surveys every table and knows just what service every one is receiving; directs the operation of his men without a word or a whisper, simply by the motion of his hand or fingers, a code of signals which he has established and taught his men. By this same method he directs, at a distance, any desired waiter or waiters to any one or more rooms in the house to take or execute orders. He disposes of a large gathering with the same tranquillity and facility as he does small ones. His management of the dining room can be characterized as PERFECT. NEATNESS and DISPATCH are the phrases used by the guest in speaking of the efficiency of the service and of the men whom he selects to serve under him.

This brilliant success as a dining room superintendent has been attributed by him to several reasons; among which may be stated: a policy always to take a deep interest in the success of the house that employs him; ever solicitous of the comfort of every patron of the house, while within the domains of his department; seeing that every one is satisfied and gets the full value of what he pays for, employing and retaining none but the most efficient, honest, industrious, intelligent, sober and polite men possible; getting for them the highest wages that can be got, and seeing to it that his men give the house in return, the best service they are capable of giving. He makes a careful study of his calling and familiarizes himself with every detail of the work in his department which he reduces to a system, and thus enables his men to perform their duty with the greatest precision and economy of time. He treats those under him with every consideration due them, and insists, as an absolute rule, on his men appearing always neat and clean, and to better enable them to do so he sells them their uniforms at cost price. He is, therefore, well liked by both the hotel managers and the patrons of the houses, and his men have for him a regard second to the strong tie of affection.

Mr. Randolph is one of the progressive men in the HEAD, SECOND AND SIDE WAITERS' NATIONAL BENEFIT ASSOCIATION, and a member of the committee of management, elected at Atlantic City, at the convention of October, 1903.

HENRY PETTIGREW,
Headwaiter, Monongahela Hotel, Pittsburg, Pa.

H. PETTIGREW.

H. Pettigrew, head waiter of the Monongahela House, Pittsburg, Pa., is one of the well known men in public life in the Smoky City, a city renowned for its many citizens of color who reside within its borders, many of whom are men of wealth and standing in the business community.

Mr. Pettigrew was born in Lexington, Rockbridge County, Va., on the 4th of March, 1865. He pursued his studies in the winter months at Harper's Ferry school, but at an early age was thrown upon his own resources to support himself. He chose the calling of a waiter and served in a subordinate capacity until his eighteenth year, at which time he had so mastered the details of his work and showed such a steadiness of character that he attracted the notice of the proprietor of a small boarding house in Virginia, who made him head waiter of his establishment.

In 1886 Mr. Pettigrew went to Blue Ridge Springs, Va., where he remained for two years. From this place he went to the Hotel Ruffner, Charleston, W. Va., where he remained for five years; then to the Gibson House, Cincinnati, Ohio, and remained there for three years. From this house he went to the Monongahela House as head waiter, where he is at present. In the fifteen years that Mr. Pettigrew has been in hotel work he has taken for his guide and motto the principle on which all life is founded—"Progress." It has always been a step higher up with him. It is a case with him of the position seeking the man and not the man seeking the position.

Mr. Pettigrew has written many pamphlets and delivered several addresses on the art of good waiting. Some of his advice to young men and women will bear quotation. He says in one of his pamphlets: 'For every man and woman there is a place in life, and having once found that place it is not good policy to leave it." "It is with a waiter as with other men, those who succeed are the ones who master all the details. If a business affords a man a livelihood, it should claim from him the best service he is capable of giving. It is the man who is faithful in a few things that stands the best chance of being some day at the head of many things."

Mr. Pettigrew believes that the future of the colored waiter depends largely on the kind of service he renders.

Mr. Pettigrew is one of the organizers of the Head, Second and Side Waiters' National Benefit Association; also one of its vice-presidents. To the young men who are entering hotel life, we would recommend them to read Mr. Pettigrew's pamphlet on the "Duty of a Waiter." Mr. Pettigrew is an object lesson of what any one can accomplish who concentrates his effort in any given direction.

A. E. JENKINS.

The State of Georgia has, no doubt, given birth to many greater sons, but to none nobler than A. E. Jenkins, who is one of the brightest stars in the hotel employment. Mr. Jenkins was born in Greenville, Mayorther County, Georgia, November 17, 1864, just at the period when the thundered roar of the cannons was clearing the clouded sky of his country, and restoring to peaceful tranquillity a united republic, and to human liberty millions of souls.

At an early age he drifted from the place where he first saw the sunlight into the West, where the atmosphere of society was more salubrious to his ambition and his manhood growth than that of his native region, and there he began his hotel career. After serving successfully as a side waiter in many of the leading hotels and mastering the art of the calling, he was promoted to the position of a second waiter in the Lindel Hotel, St. Louis. From there he went to the Palmer House, Chicago, Ill., and thence to the Ryar Hotel, St. Paul, Minn.

After serving in these, three of the leading hotels of the West, in the capacity of a second waiter, he felt confident that the elements in him necessary to be a successful head waiter had been sufficiently developed and, therefore, he was fitted to take up the task and assume the responsibility of superintending the dining room, hence he accepted the position of head waiter at the Centropolis Hotel, Kansas City, Mo. He remained there for six years. At the end of which, having given ample satisfaction, he was requested by the same management to take charge and open their new hotel at Indianapolis, Ind., "The New English," conducted on both the European and American plans. Both dining rooms were under his direct supervision; with a crew of forty-two waiters, three bussmen and two assistants. He gave to these dining rooms a service which will long be remembered with pleasure by those who had the good fortune to dine there.

After three years at this hotel, he received an offer, more to his advantage, to take charge of the Albany Hotel, Denver, Colo., which he accepted; like the New English, this hotel also ran both system of dining rooms, which were under his superintendency, with a crew of

46 COMMANDERS OF THE DINING ROOM

Respt yours A. E. Jenkins

Headwaiter Hotel McKinley, Canton, Ohio.

twenty-eight side men and two bussmen. Over the dining rooms of this house he presided for one year, with credit to himself and financial advantage to the management. Leaving this hotel, he went to the Coats House, Kansas City; having charge there also of its American and European dining rooms, with forty-two side waiters, three bussmen and three assistants. He remained with this house for twelve months.

Mr. Jenkins being thoroughly conversant with the European and American plans of dining room service, when the Bailey Catering Co., of Buffalo, N. Y., during the Pan-American Exposition, in 1901, was in need of a capable man to take charge of its dining rooms of the the largest European restaurant on the Exposition grounds, he was selected as the man best fitted to fill the position. His genius for managing men and handling large bodies of people, was well tested during the Exposition. At its close, Mr. Jenkins went to the Ruffner Hotel, Charleston, W. Va., where he remained until December, 1903, at which time he left to take charge of the (new) Hotel McKinley, Canton, Ohio.

He has given perfect satisfaction to every one of the houses he has served, and from every one he holds first class references. To Mr. Willis Howe, superintendent of the Palmer House, Chicago, Ill., he can refer, particularly.

Everything that tends to, and concerns the progress of the race to which he belongs, interests him. He is a Past Grand Chancellor and Past Supreme Representative of the Knights of Pythias, and a thirty-second degree Mason; a member also of the A. M. E. Bethel connection.

Nature has been very kind and indulgent with Mr. Jenkins, as it has given him a very pleasant physique to look upon and a well developed and commanding stature of five feet, eleven and a half inches, with a weight of 245 pounds of flesh to his credit. In conjunction with these, like many others of his kinsmen in this calling, he possesses basic elements which, had circumstances been otherwise, to have permitted their natural growth and full development, judging him under an oppressive social condition, would make him to-day or some day to come, an important factor in one of the higher callings in the world's material civilization.

However, he is not disposed to grumble at his lot. He makes the best of life as he meets it, and contenting and consoling himself, like many others, with the fact that man is but a child of circumstances, and that the force of circumstances dominate the nation the same alike as it does the man, therefore that what he may not do to-day, when the circuit of years shall have lapsed into decades, his progeny will surely do to-morrow. For it is just as easy for the ingenuity of man battling against the force of nature to successfully obliterate the light of day, as to forever, by oppressive acts, cruel sentiments and mere human will, retard from full growth ten million acorns imbedded in the fertile soil of nature's earth, or tens of millions of God's created souls with human heart, energy and will.

WALTER C. OUTLAW.

In the year 1857 Walter C. Outlaw was born in the small town of Windsor, N. C. There he remained until he was fifteen years of age. In the summer of 1872 he determined to make a livelihood for himself and to contribute to the support of his parents. Having received their consent he set out for the north with no definite idea as to where he was going or where he intended to settle. He, however, reached Mattapoisett, Mass., and after remaining there for two weeks resolved to go to New Bedford. At this place he was fortunate in getting a position as a side waiter in the Parker House, where he remained until 1881. His next engagement was with a private family as a butler, where he remained until 1885.

In the fall of 1885, desiring to see more of the country, Mr. Outlaw secured employment with the Pullman Palace Car Company, and remained with it until the year 1891. In the spring of this year he went to the Union League Club, New York City, to work as a side waiter and remained until 1895, and, in the summer of the same year, he accepted the position of second waiter under Mr. E. W. Harper at the Prospect House, Bay Shore, L. I., and returned with him again in 1896. In the summer of the following year he went with Mr. Harper as second in command of the Rockingham Hotel, Narragansett Pier. As years roll along the mile stones of progress, as a rule, in the career of a progressive man increase, and thus it was with Mr. Outlaw, for in the following summer (1898) he had grown to a state of efficiency which elevated him to the commandership of the dining room of the Rockingham. The summers of 1899 and 1900 found him in charge of the dining room of the Mansion House, Brooklyn, N. Y.

Travel as we may, we sometimes return to our starting point to stay, and thus in the fall of 1900 Mr. Outlaw is found to have completed the circuit and returned to the point from which he started in life—the Parker House.

Life's journey is an up hill climb.

But he who has the will power is sure to conquer in time.

Mr. Outlaw has been signally fortunate in the fact that he has never been discharged from any of his places. He is ever attentive to duty and a strict disciplinarian; always putting forth his greatest

Walter C. Outlaw,
Headwaiter, Parker House, New Bedford, Mass.

efforts to obtain the best results in whatever he undertakes to do. He works always with the motto of David Crockett before him: "Be sure you are right and then go ahead." He is a man of marked individuality and is considered one of the most successful and progressive head waiters of the present day. He is an active member of the Head, Second and Side Waiters' National Benefit Association.

Mr. Outlaw is blessed in having a very accomplished lady for his wife, who takes pride in the success of her husband and cheers him on to higher things.

W. P. Landon
Headwaiter Reade House, Chattanooga, Tenn.

W. P. LANDON.

W. P. Landon was born on the 22nd day of September, 1867, in Newman, Ga. In 1884, he selected hotel life for a calling and entered the employ of the proprietor of the Grand Hotel, Atlanta, Ga. His first position was that of silver washer, at which he remained until the fall of 1885. Since then, he has advanced through all the grades up to that of head waiter. His record is as follows: Two years at Café Kattenhorn and Vignaux, Atlanta, Ga.; one year and a half at Folsom's Café, Atlanta; six and a half years at the Portland, Portland, Oregon, at which place he was second waiter for part of the time. For a short time head waiter at the Majestic, Atlanta; one year at the Southern Hotel, Chattanooga, Tenn.; six months at the Rathburn Hotel, Jacksonville, Fla.; and at the present time head waiter at the Read House, Chattanooga, Tenn., at which place he has been for nearly three years.

Mr. Landon was married to Miss Ella Edith Perdue, on August 21st, 1895 and has a comfortable home in Chattanooga. He believes that a man in public life ought to be married, because the sympathetic companionship and refining influence of a wife are the best rewards that a man can have after the worry of a long day, as it tends to make him more settled.

Mr. Landon is a member of the Head, Second and Side Waiters' National Benefit Association, and is an active worker in his section of the country in making known the objects of the Association and in every way advancing its interests.

There is no doubt, with his energy and push, the future has in store for him much greater success than he has already achieved. Process of time might yet place him among the progressive business men of the Sunny South—that great theatre in which his race has and is further destined to play a great part in its material development, both as employees and employers. The years of travel through the wilderness will fully prepare them to undertake the industrial and commercial responsibilities which are gradually being developed.

The sagacity displayed by Mr. Landon and many of the other men in the calling, gives evidence of a bright future; for the natural laws of political economy in this very material world in which we live, will, in the last analysis, separate the bubble from the solid substance, and that force which has been stored up by the wisdom of strict economy, will be the most important factor in the life and death struggle for existence.

C. M. FARRAR.

Treasurer Head, Second and Side Waiters' National Benefit Association.
Headwaiter Merchant Club, Baltimore, Md.

CALVIN M. FARRAR.

Calvin M. Farrar was born in the city of "brotherly love"—Philadelphia. The South can point with reasonable pride to the long list of men whose names have gone down in history as head waiters, and who knew the technique of their profession long before the introduction in this country of white men in the dining rooms of first-class hotels. It has been asserted that, with very few exceptions, all the men who have risen to the position of head waiters throughout the country came from the South. While this is true, in the case of Mr. Farrar we have one of the exceptions.

At the age of fourteen Mr. Farrar left Philadelphia for North Carolina with a man named Smith, who had raised him from a small boy. In North Carolina he obtained employment in a grocery store as errand boy. Being of a studious disposition, and having plenty of time to indulge his craving for knowledge, he spent his leisure hours in pouring over his books. Much of his spare time was also utilized in teaching his less fortunate companions how to read and write, for from a boy he was deeply impressed with the condition of his race, especially in the South. This inclination to do everything in his power to help every deserving member of his race is still a dominant feature of Mr. Farrar, for he believes that ignorance is the handmaid of vice and everything that is bad, but that intelligence properly directed is a power.

Mr. Farrar's first experience in hotel life was at the old National Hotel, Washington, D. C., where he was a bell boy. Then he became a scullion in the kitchen. He rose by sheer strength of his personality and natural ability in this hotel, from the position of scullion to that of a waiter in the nurse's hall, then to bussman, then to that of a waiter in the dining-room, and then to second waiter. While holding the last position he left and went to Long Branch, N. J., for the season. At the close of the season he went West for a short time, but not liking the life out there, he returned to Washington, where he met Mr. H. Z. Sykes, who engaged him as second waiter for the Mount Vernon. Subsequently he was promoted to the position of head waiter. He remained at the Mount Vernon until 1882, when he accepted the superintendency of the dining-room of the

Merchants' Club, Baltimore, Md., a position he has held for twenty-one years. This is a great record.

Mr. Farrar's position in Baltimore is an unique one. He knows and is known to every prominent merchant, banker and broker in that city, and it is doubtful whether there is a colored man who is more highly respected in the community than he is, or whose influence is greater or whose credit is better. The list of his employments shows that he has the power of adhesion highly developed, for he sticks to a place and does not let go until the place lets him go.

Mr. Farrar is a member of the Head and Second Waiters' National Benefit Association and was its vice-president for three successive terms. At the convention held in Washington, D. C., 1902, he was placed on the Board of Directors, and has since been elected treasurer at the convention held at Atlantic City, N. J., October, 1903. He is a thirty-second degree Scottish Rites Mason.

The work of such men will ultimately tell in the material advancement of their race. May they multiply more and more.

GEORGE A. CURRY.

George A. Curry, who for a number of years has made his home in the beautiful little village of Demarest, N. J., was born in Milford, Kent County, Delaware, on October 1st, 1855.

After attending the public schools for several years and acquiring a fairly good education, he began to consider the importance of looking forward to some vocation to which he could best adapt himself. Having made up his mind to venture out into the world for himself, he one day, told his mother of his intentions. But she, like most mothers, was bitterly opposed to his leaving home, as he was scarcely seventeen years of age. Not discouraged, however, by her kindly persuasion, he approached his father, who gave him more encouragement; so they talked the matter over and with much reluctance on his mother's part they decided to let him make a trial.

Though but a lad of seventeen years, he decided to go to Philadelphia in search of a friend, whom he knew was employed in a hotel there. With a very limited knoweldg of traveling, and no idea even of the city of his destination, he undertook the journey alone. On arriving in Philadelphia, he was fortunate in meeting a man who was acquainted with the party whom he was seeking. This person was extremely courteous and kind to him and directed him to the residence of the friend who was very much surprised on seeing him; not having any knowledge of his intended visit. However, everything worked in his favor, and the following morning he secured employment at the Washington Hotel, then situated on the corner of 7th and Chestnut streets, as hall man, at a salary of $15.00 per month. As Mr. Curry expressed it, "This looked like a fortune to me." He remained there about six months as hall man.

Having a great desire to become a waiter, he became more persistent in his efforts to fulfil his ambition, and in order to attain his desire, he accepted a position as dish carrier in the same hotel, remaining on watch every day from twelve to one o'clock, in order that he might gather some knowledge of the duties of a waiter. After a little while, he thought that he could wait as well as some of the other men, and so a trial was given him, but he very soon realized that he was much mistaken. His first experience was sufficient to discourage

GEORGE A. CURRY,
Headwaiter, Congress Hall, Saratoga Springs, N. Y., and the new St. Charles, New Orleans, La.

him in any further pursuit. Having received an order amidst much excitement and bustle, before he could reach the kitchen he had entirely forgotten everything that had been ordered. Even this, however, did not cool the ardor of his ambition to succeed.

The next day he did much better and so steadily improved. The following year he made a change, going to Plainfield, N. J., to work in a summer hotel. Of course, being a new man he was assigned to wait on the family, yet he cared not where he was placed, for he had fully made up his mind to accomplish something, regardless of the many seemingly insurmountable obstacles that confronted him.

One day, to his great surprise, the proprietor of the hotel called the head waiter, and said to him, in the presence of young Curry: "Give this waiter a family, he is too good a man to wait on the officer's table."

Naturally Mr. Curry was much elated at this mark of appreciation of his services, and from that day his success was assured; he began gradually, to climb step by step from one success to another, until he became a second waiter under Mr. Thomas Smith in 1876, and filled that position with much credit for two seasons. In 1879, he was engaged to take charge as head waiter of the Haynes Hotel, Springfield, Mass.; filling the position there until the spring of 1881. He then returned to New York to take charge of the old St. Mark's Hotel, New Brighton, Staten Island, where he remained in charge for two seasons. In 1883 he accepted the charge of the Colorado Hotel, 726 Broadway, New York, and remained until 1885, when he was engaged by the well-known head waiter, Mr. Hiram S. Thomas, to go to Saratoga with him, to open the Grand Union Hotel for the summer. From the Grand Union, he went with Mr. Thomas to open the famous Lakewood Hotel, at Lakewood, N. J., where he remained for five seasons. It was about this time that he accepted the position as head waiter at the Congress Hall Hotel, at Saratoga Springs, N. Y., which position he has filled successfully for twelve seasons, and over which dining room he still presides. In the year 1896, he accepted the position of head waiter of the new St. Charles Hotel, New Orleans, La., opening it in January of the same year. He has had charge of this hotel ever since, remaining there from October until the first of June, when he leaves his second man in charge, and returns to the Congress Hall, Saratoga Springs, N. Y., for the summer season.

This is, indeed, a remarkable career, and proves that patience and persistency, coupled with an earnest endeavor, bring their reward in ultimate success. Mr. Curry is undoubtedly a man of great ability and would be a success in almost any of the higher callings. However, there is no telling to what height he might yet climb in the industrial world. The branch of the human family to which he belongs has a great future in this country, regardless of the difficulties which confront it and which in conquering, merely develops the intellect and strengthens its manhood. Its possibilities are unlimited, possessing a commercial and financial potentiality greater than many an individual nation's, in its annual expenditure of over five hundred million dollars.

The executive ability of Mr. Curry that has manifested itself during his career, might yet be used in concentrating and utilizing this great power to the greater material advancement of his race.

RICHARD JONES WILDER.

The subject of this sketch was born near Petersburg, Chesterfield County, Va., on March 16th, 1848. His parents were Adam and Jennie Lee Wilder. The elder Wilder in early life was a successful farmer and later became a caterer. It was under his father that young Wilder began his career. The elder Wilder gained quite a reputation as a successful caterer. He gave his attention to the serving of dinners, preparing banquets, barbecues, etc. There was seldom a noted affair in his section of the country in which he was not called upon to officiate. His son, Richard Jones Wilder, showed early ability in the line of the business which his father followed and in which he was himself destined to become prominent. He was of great assistance to his father, for with his original imagination and progressive disposition he was constantly seeing and suggesting some new improvement in the line of service. He early manifested those sterling qualities ot head and heart which have made him one of the ablest as well as one of the most amiable and popular men in the hotel business.

Mr. Wilder worked with his father until he was nineteen years old, at which time his father died. Left to his own resources, young Wilder went as a side waiter, in 1872, to the old Commonwealth Hotel, now the Langham, of Boston, Mass. He served there in this capacity for three winters. His first experience as a second waiter was in the summer of 1873 at the Ocean House, Old Orchard Beach, Me. In 1874 he was appointed head waiter at the Rose Standish House, Downer's Landing, Mass., serving there for six summers, dividing his time in the winters of this period between New York and Boston as head or second waiter in various houses.

Since then he has always been head, second or third waiter, except for a short period when, as a matter of choice and for a change from official responsibility, he waited on the side. Among the houses he has served as head waiter are Hotel Wellesley, Wellesley, Mass., two seasons; the Brunswick and Copley Square, Boston, Mass., the former, two years, and the latter three winters. As second waiter, the St. James, Jacksonville, Fla.; Magnolia Hotel, Magnolia, Fla.; Royal Poinciana, Palm Beach, Fla., and the Homestead, Hot Springs, Va. In all of these varied capacities he has given eminent satisfaction to the guests, and to his official superiors.

R. J. WILDER.
Headwaiter Farragut House, Rye Beach, N. H.

There is one thing remarkable about Mr. Wilder, and that is during his long career of thirty years and more—twenty years of which he has served in some official capacity, he has shown the same exactness, fidelity and scrupulous care for the interests of every one under whom he served as characterized him when in charge for himself. He has never been charged by any head waiter with designs on his position or with working against him, or with any of those mean tricks which are known in hotel parlance as "throwing him down." Wherever he has worked, he has always retained the esteem of his employers and the respect of the men working under him. Perhaps the best proof of Mr. Wilder's business ability, tact and executive management is the long period which has marked his superintendency of the dining room of the Farragut House, Rye Beach, N. H. For eleven successive summers he has been in charge of this exclusive and eminently respectable resort. The high character of this house may be best judged from the fact that it never advertises. For months before the opening every room in the house is taken; in fact, some persons make arrangements as early as January, and in the case of regulars it is common for the same rooms to be engaged from season to season. The hotel has always been noted for its exclusiveness, and none but the highest class of people go there. Its founder, the late John P. Philbrick, was a representative of that staid old New England type of respectability which has given us some of the highest and best types of American citizenship.

It has been no light undertaking to fill as acceptably as Mr. Wilder has filled, the position of head waiter for a house so exacting; and his successive engagements is the best testimony to his efficiency.

It is significant that of all the hotels on the North Shore, the Farragut is the only one that now employs colored waiters.

Mr. Wilder belongs to that old school of head waiters that are fast passing away—Thomas, Booker, Lucas and a host of others have passed on and gone to join the ranks of that "innumerable caravan." They were great men in their day and generation. Mr. Wilder, in commenting upon the decadence of the colored waiters, says: "It is a subject that furnishes us with much food for thought."

Like most of the men of the old regime, Mr. Wilder had only limited opportunities for education. Born in the time of travail and trouble, with the gaunt spectre of war casting its darkening shadows over the country, he had little chance and less opportunity for books. While yet scarcely at his majority, the black cloud of war, which had been hovering for years, bursted in all its fury, and the red-handed demon of blood and carnage ruled the country. When this had passed, and peace once more reigned over the land, Mr. Wilder took up the serious problem of life. He attended private school in Petersburg, and later went to night school in Boston, and one winter at the then V. N. & C. I., and two winters at Boydton Institute. This completed his school education. Though starting late in life and retarded by many handicaps, Mr. Wilder persevered, and his life is an example which the young men of to-day might emulate with profit. He is a devout Christian and a faithful member of the A. M. E. Zion connection. He is a charter member of Plymouth Rock Lodge 1622, G. U. O. of O. F., constituted in 1874 and located in Boston, Mass.

JOHN A. GLOSTER.

John A. Gloster, of whom we now write, is at present head waiter at the Sterling Hotel, Wilkesbarre, Pa., where he has been for the past five or six years.

He was born in the little town of Berlin, Ontario, Canada, on December 23, 1868. His early education was received in the Canadian schools. His first work in the hotel life was in the Queen's Hotel, Toronto, Canada, where he was employed as a bell boy and where he remained for about six years.

It was while working as a bell boy there that he learned something of the dining room service, as every bell boy was required to have an apron and a jacket, and be in readiness to assist in a dining room rush.

While working there, he became desirous of learning something of the life in different hotels, and thus gain a more extensive experience in the dining room work. Consequently he left the Queen's Hotel and went to Detroit, Michigan, where he secured the position of captain of the stand in the Russell House; from there he went to the Cadillac, thence to the Normandie. But afterwards he became restless and decided to visit the different States of this country. He, therefore, went to Montreal, Canada, and obtained the position of porter with the Pullman Palace Car Company, and remained with this company about two years and six months. Concluding that he had learned all he could in such employment and finding nothing in it, but hard work and poor pay, he resolved to return to hotel life, and accepted a position as head bell man in the Tift House, Buffalo, New York, where he remained about one year and six months. While there, he decided to select dining room work for his career, having already had some experience in such well-known hotels as the Cadillac, the Normandie in Detroit, and the Royal, in Hamilton, Ontario, Canada, in his younger days. He, therefore, applied to the manager of the Mansion House, at Buffalo, New York, who gave him the position of record waiter. This hotel had the reputation of setting the finest table of any hotel in that city. There he remained for about two years. From there he went to the Hotel Jermyn, Scranton, Pa., as record waiter, where he did service for another two years.

In December, 1898, Mr. Gloster accepted the position of head

JOHN A. GLOSTER,
Headwaiter, Hotel Sterling, Wilkes Barre, Pa.

waiter of the Sterling Hotel, Wilkesbarre, Pa. There he still remains. Though the house has changed hands, and many discharges made in every department, the new management in taking charge of the hotel in January, 1901, soon realized his worth and expressed themselves as highly pleased with the working of his department and therefore retained him as head waiter.

Mr. Gloster says, "I find it no easy matter to properly conduct a first-class dining room. As a matter of fact, I can only ascribe my success to the strict discipline I maintain, and the intelligent and well-trained waiters which I employ. I will not keep any man with bad moral character, because I feel it a duty not only to employ first-class waiters, but also those possessing good character. Naturally we sometimes employ waiters who prove themselves worthless, especially after they have received their first month's pay; but I am opposed to giving such men employment, and as soon as I can secure another waiter I discharge a worthless one.

"We, as managers of the dining room, owe it to ourselves as well as to the proprietors of the hotels that the standing of the dining room service be in every respect first-class.

"Moreover, I believe that every head and second waiter should secure the different hotel weeklies, in order that they may keep abreast of events in their line of service and thus be strictly up-to-date. I also believe in instructing my men in the art of service, and therefore I hold a school every Friday evening."

Mr. Gloster is a member of the Head, Second and Side Waiters' National Benefit Association, and considers it an excellent organization for advancing the service, and so he hopes that the members of the Association will do all in their power to bring the hotel dining room service up to the highest possible standard of merit.

W. R. Harris,
Headwaiter.

W. R. HARRIS.

A son of the land of sunshine and sweet magnolia, W. R. Harris, late of the Hotel McKinley, Canton, Ohio, is a man whose record stands A1 in the hotel world. He is known all over the south and southwestern parts of this country as a man who employs the best men in his dining room. The people who visit his house go away with a pleasant recollection of good and intelligent service from the rank and file of the men who are under the eagle eye of this capable director. Mr. Harris is often applied to by hotel managers to recommend young men for positions as head and second waiters, because they say they like to get a man who has worked under him. This in itself is a strong recommendation.

Mr. Harris was born in Andover county, Va., in 1864. He went to school at Ashland, Va., but the best part of his education was obtained at a night school at Tarboro, N. C., for at seven years of age he was placed in a private family by his mother "to keep (as she said) the flies off the table." This was his induction into the dining room, and he has since passed through every degree in the service of hotel waiter, until to-day he is a past master in the art of waiting.

Mr. Harris has been head waiter of the Carroll, of Vicksburg, Miss.; the Hollenden, of Cleveland, Ohio, and at Buffalo; the Mt. Vernon Hotel, at Mt. Vernon; the St. James and the Rennert, of Baltimore; the Colonade and the Gladstone, of Philadelphia; the Louisville Hotel, Louisville, Ky., and the Bennett House, Cincinnati, Ohio. Some of these hotels are conducted on the European plan and some on the American plan. So it can be seen that Mr. Harris is well equipped in every way to uphold the dignity and traditions of his calling. As a friend he is sincere and warm hearted, and as a companion he is genial and instructive, for his reminiscences are replete with only the best experiences of a calling which has brought him in contact with some of the brightest of America's sons. Being possessed of a mind which absorbs all that is good, Mr. Harris's path through life is one of sunshine which cannot but help to shed its rays on all those with whom he comes in contact.

He is a very progressive man and inspires those under him with enthusiasm and ambition to succeed.

JAMES L. DICKERSON.
Headwaiter, Bedell House, Pittsburgh, Pa.

JAMES L. DICKERSON.

James L. Dickerson was born in Richmond, Va., on May 12th, 1858. His parents being slaves, he was raised by Lawyer J. P. Pleasant, of Richmond, Va.

Unfortunately Mr. Dickerson's chances for acquiring an education in early life were poor, but realizing what he had missed, he in later years attended night school in Boston, and thus made up for what he had lost in early years.

At the age of fifteen, he started to work as waiter in the Old Exchange and Ballard Hotel at Richmond, Va. In 1880 he went to Boston, Mass., and in 1881 on leaving Boston, went to Long Branch, N. J., where he was made an officer in the dining room of the Howland Hotel, under Mr. Frank P. Thompson.

At the close of the season of 1882, Mr. Dickerson returned to Boston and became valet to Mr. A. P. Porter. During his stay with this gentleman, Mr. Dickerson made four trips to Europe, and spent upwards of two years in traveling over the European countries.

The greater portion of this time, however, was spent in Paris, and because of this he naturally acquired a knowledge of the language; consequently Mr. Dickerson speaks the French language very fluently.

After his first trip, which was made in 1883, he became united in marriage to Miss Ella Hart, of Baltimore, who, however, died in Boston in 1890, leaving to Mr. Dickerson the care of a son.

Returning to Boston after leaving the employ of Mr. Potter he took up waiting as a calling, and has followed it up to the present time.

For six years Mr. Dickerson was head waiter at the Woodland Park Hotel, Auburndale, Mass.; four years head waiter at the Hotel Nottingham, in Boston, while the remainder of his time in Boston was spent as head waiter at the American House.

Mr. Dickerson is known as one of the leading head waiters in New England. He manages his dining room and the men under him with much skill, and by a well developed system, coupled with his ability for getting up extra French dishes, and managing dinner parties, he has largely added to his reputation as a head waiter. He is very frequently spoken of as "The Born Head Waiter."

On May 15th, 1902, Mr. Dickerson took charge as head waiter at the Hotel Rennert, Baltimore, Md., which position he is still occupying.

Mr. Dickerson, after remaining a widower for upwards of twelve years, became imbued with the desire for a life partner, and thereby made his second matrimonial venture by taking in marriage Mrs. M. A. Penn, of Clifton Forge, Va. Mr. and Mrs. Dickerson now make their home in Baltimore.

Mr. Dickerson is tall and well proportioned; is easy-going and possesses an elegance of carriage and bearing. In manners, he is exceedingly polite and agreeable. In him one sees not only the efficient and intelligent head waiter, but the cultured and polished man. He is thoroughly conversant with every feature of dining room etiquette.

JOSEPH THORNTON LEE.

Joseph Thornton Lee was born in Loudoun county, Virginia, on the 17th of June, 1852. His early life was spent on the farms in his native county. Even in those days his power of leadership was so much in evidence that long before reaching manhood, he was placed in full charge of one of the largest farms in Virginia. Had the opportunity presented itself, and the colored youth had had as much social and moral support and encouragement as a white youth with the same endowments, he may have been as foremost in the mechanical world as he is to-day in the hotel world, for he early manifested an aptitude amounting to genius in the handling of intricate machinery, being able to put together any complicated machine which had been shipped to the farm in separate parts. His life of drudgery without the hope of advancement was, however, not congenial to a man of Mr. Lee's temperament and capacity. He felt that there was a force within him which needed better opportunity for its development. He, therefore decided to leave the farm and seek some other field of employment. The hotel doors seemed to offer the least force of resistance, hence he decided to enter there, believing that it afforded better opportunity. His first experience in this calling took place in a country tavern in Moorefield, W. Va. There he worked from 1873 to 1876. In those days, and in that part of the country, a waiter had to do everything, from cleaning boots to currying a horse. He next found employment in a hotel in Deerpark, Md., and soon began to show his great grasp of business affairs and sound judgment, which have since made him one of the foremost head waiters of America.

While at Deerpark it was Mr. Lee's good fortune to serve and attract the notice of such men as General U. S. Grant, who stopped at this place on the eve of his departure on his trip around the world; and the late Robert Garrett, president of the B. & O. R. R. From Deerpark he went to Oakland, Md., and in 1877 to the National Hotel, Washington, D. C. In 1878 he went to the Grand Union Hotel, Saratoga. At this place, those early traits of character which have already been referred to in this sketch, at once found a chance to manifest themselves, and one year after Mr. Lee entered this house he was promoted to the official position as

Joseph T. Lee.

Headwaiter Grand Union, Saratoga Springs, and Hotel Chamberlain, Old Point Comfort, Va.

head in the nurses' hall. As if by magic, the shyness and awkwardness of the country youth disappeared, and in its stead appeared the modest and polished man, liberal and fair-minded in his dealings, and with an individuality that has attracted every one to him, and makes him the ideal superintendent of the dining room. Such merit did he exhibit in his first minor official position that in the winter of the same year, he was called to the Metropolitan Hotel, New York, as second waiter under headwaiter Hiram S. Thomas. He retained this position for three years, and during the summer months when Mr. Thomas was away in Saratoga, took entire charge of the dining room. In 1882 he was given full charge of the Metropolitan, which position he held until 1887, when he was chosen by Mr. J. M. Otter, manager of the hotels owned by the estate of A. T. Stewart, as head waiter of the Grand Union, Saratoga, and has been in charge of this large hotel up to the present time.

In 1890 Mr. Lee opened the Union League Club in Brooklyn, N. Y., where he remained for two winters, going from there to the De Soto, in Savannah, Ga. This place he held during the winter months until 1898, when he was called to the Chamberlain Hotel, at Old Point Comfort, Va., under the new management.

Mr. Lee's reputation is national; he stands at the head of his profession as the presiding genius over two of the largest houses in the world. He has so mastered the technique of his business, that it may safely be said without comparisons, that he may have equals, but no superiors. He is very popular with his men, though a strict disciplinarian whose methods are standard examples for all who wish to succeed. Such a man is deserving of all the praise that can be bestowed on him, for he elevates not only himself, but those about him. If every head waiter were like him, there would be to-day a greater demand for their services in the metropolis of the country.

Like all great men who have obtained what learning they have by overcoming obstacles, Mr. Lee is a great lover of education, and is ever ready to extend a helping hand to any deserving young man who is ambitious to procure a good education. He spares no expense in the education of his children, and thus his oldest daughter, a young lady of twenty-one, has successfully passed all the grades in the Public Schools of New York, and for the past three years has been one of the most successful teachers in the Public Schools in the Borough of Brooklyn.

In 1880 Mr. Lee married Miss Mildred Turner, of Clarksburg, W. Va. To them ten children have been born, and like the mother of the Gracchi, Mrs. Lee points with pride to her children as her jewels.

He possesses a very beautiful home on Madison street, Brooklyn, and is besides the owner of several other valuable parcels of real estate in that city.

Mr. Lee joined the order of Free Masons in the year 1884, and is a member of Hiram No. 4, N. Y. He is also a Royal Arch Mason, Knight Templar, Past Eminent Commander of his Commandery, Past Commander of Paul Dayton Commandry, and Past Generalissimo of New York State. He received the thirty-third degree, the Scottish Rite degree, and is also Nobleman of the Mystic Shrine, and has "trod the hot sand." For two years he was president of the United Literary Society of Saratoga, N. Y., and declined through stress of circumstances to accept a third term. He is now president of the Frederic Douglass Literary Association of Saratoga, an office he has held for years. His work, in this office, has been far-reaching. Through his untiring efforts the association has become one of the leading institutions of its kind. During his administration the association has given financial aid to many worthy schools in the South, and has donated largely to the charitable institutions of Saratoga.

Such is the life of a great self-made man, one of Nature's able men. A man whose life is stainless, and a life that can be pointed to as an example for young men to emulate. His success is due to close observance of business, and learning the characteristics of different people with whom he has to deal.

WM. S. FOREMAN.

Wm. S. Foreman was born in the Dominion of Canada. His parents Isaac and Frances Foreman, were natives of the Southern States, but went to Canada in the fifties and settled down in Hamilton, Ontario, where the subject of this sketch was born on February 2nd, 1856. Later on his parents moved further West, and made their home in Brantford, where young Foreman passed the greater part of his early age. He attended the public schools and received a good common school education. On leaving school he secured employment in a milk and dairy establishment. In this occupation he worked for some time. Finally, however, he gave it up and went and learned the trade of a painter and paper-hanger. This he followed with much success. Having a desire to travel, he left home. Finding some difficulties, however, in securing work at his trade, because of unreasonable prejudice, he turned his attention to the hotel occupation, as one affording the best opportunity. He first started as private doorman, in the Queen's Hotel, Toronto, Can. There he remained for six months, at the end of which time desiring to visit the Southern States, young Foreman left and went to Norfolk, Va., where he had some relatives residing. He arrived there in 1878; and after a while, finding that his funds were becoming low, he bethought himself to seek some employment. Failing again to procure employment at his trade, he once more turned to the hotel service of which he knew but very little. Through the kindness, however, of Mr. R. S. Dodson, then the proprietor of the Atlantic Hotel, who took a fancy to him, Mr. Foreman was given work in the dining room. This was his initiation into the service with jacket and apron, and thus he began his career in the calling. Being very apt he learned quickly and remained at this place for two years.

Like every progressive young man, he longed for a larger field in which to operate and to learn more of the details of the business, and also of the manners and peculiarities of other people. So he set out and ultimately found himself at Old Point Comfort, where he secured employment in the Hygeia Hotel, where he remained until the fall, when he went to the city of Washington, and entered the service of the Ebbitt House. Disliking the atmosphere of Washington, he was soon after on his way North. On reaching the city of Troy, N. Y., he soon

WM. S. FOREMAN.
Headwaiter, International Hotel, Niagara Falls, N. Y.

obtained employment in the Troy House, remaining there for but a short period. He afterwards went to Richfield Springs, N. Y., and entered the service of the Spring House. At the close of the season he went to Albany, and worked in the Kenmore House, during the winter, going from there in the spring, to the International Hotel, Niagara Falls. Going back to Albany, he entered the dining room of the Delevan House, during the winter of 1880, as side waiter, but soon after was given the place as second in command and succeeded to the head waiter's position in 1882. He held this position for twelve and a half years, when he resigned and entered the hotel business as a proprietor, opening the Windsor Hotel, in Maiden Lane, Albany, N. Y., which he conducted until 1896, when the sad misfortune in the death of his wife, caused him to sell out. During the period of his proprietorship, he superintended the dining room of the International Hotel, at Niagara Falls in the summer months.

On the loss of his wife he left Albany and returned to the land of his nativity (Canada), where he made his home for nine years, but continued service in the hotels of the States, having charge as head waiter, of such well-known houses as the Regent, Washington, D. C., for three years; the Broezel, Buffalo, N. Y., and the Vanderbilt, Syracuse, N. Y. Going to Florida in 1903, to the hotel Indian River, Rockledge. In this interested and successful career of twenty-two years in the service, Mr. Foreman has evidenced great ability for mastering details which, if utilized in other callings, would, no doubt, bring him greater remuneration. He is progressive and intelligent; possesses very strongly, the elements of success. He is a member of the Head, Second and Side Waiters' National Benefit Association.

J. H. HOLMES,
Headwaiter, Post Tavern, Battle Creek, Mich.

J. H. HOLMES.

J. H. Holmes was born in Warsaw, Mo., on the 12th of December, 1856. His father died when he was quite a child, leaving his mother with a large family dependent upon her for support.

On the 7th of April, 1870, his widowed mother moved to Lawrence, Kansas, where young Holmes obtained work on a farm. His whole ambition was to obtain enough money to purchase a home for his dear mother and to assist in the education of his brothers and sisters, which he accomplished.

Mr. Holmes always speaks of his mother as his "guiding star" and his "prayer is that God will spare her for a long time to remain with him."

In June, 1876, he went to work as a water-boy in the Eldredge House in Lawrence. After six months he was given a table, and three years later, he obtained the position of head waiter of the McClure House, Canon City, Colo. Since then he has had charge of some of the leading hotels in the West, notably, the Cliff House, at Manitou, Colo.; the American in Denver; the Denver Club; the Murray in Omaha, Neb.; in all of which he installed his own crew. He was captain of the morning watch at the Milliard in 1892, and resigned to take charge of the dining room of the Grand at Council Bluffs, Ia. Closing the season at the Grand in September, 1893, he opened the Koehler, at Grand Rapids, Neb., on October 1st. From this hotel he resigned in September, 1894, to re-open the Grand at Council Bluffs. He remained at the Grand until December 14th, 1900 and then reported for duty at the Post Tavern, Battle Creek, Mich., on the 16th of December of the same year, at which place he has remained as head waiter up to the present time.

Mr. Holmes has worked for his present employer, Mr. E. F. Clark, at different times in the capacity of head waiter, and the feeling which exists between them is one of mutual good will, for each feels that the other is fair and upright in all his dealings, and that the effort of one to make the service of the hotel a success is ably seconded by the other. This is as it should be.

Mr. Holmes is ably assisted in his duties by Mr. A. W. Johnson, his second waiter, and a crew of twenty men of whom he speaks very highly and says he could not have succeeded had he not received the loyal co-operation of his men.

GEORGE H. RICHARDSON,
Headwaiter, Columbus, Ohio.

GEORGE H. RICHARDSON.

George H. Richardson, the subject of this sketch, is what may be termed a self-made man. He was born in Spartansburg, S. C., on the 1st day of May, 1867. Both of his parents died when he was in his early teens. He therefore was compelled to leave school and earn a living not only for himself, but to aid in the maintenance of three sisters. His first employment was in a baker's establishment, which he entered as an apprentice; he remained there until he had mastered the trade—an accomplishment which has been of great assistance to him in the vocation which he has since followed. His first initiation in hotel work was in his native city, where he soon climbed to the top, for in a few years he became head waiter and steward at a summer resort in Saluda, N. C. Remaining there for two seasons, he accepted a tempting offer to go to Richmond, Va., as cook at one of the leading houses, where he remained for quite a period. On leaving he went to Cleveland, Ohio, where he employed the knowledge gained in the bakery, by opening a general catering business. Here he became known to the hotel managers and proprietors as a man who knew his business from the bottom to the top and therefore when the Stillman changed from white to colored help, Mr. Richardson was engaged as second waiter, and later promoted to the position of head waiter.

So far he has been very successful and demonstrates great ability in mastering the art of his calling.

Mr. Richardson has been a member of the Head, Second and Side Waiters' Benefit Association since its organization in 1899. At the meeting in Buffalo he was elected vice-president for Ohio and was re-elected at the convention held in Washington, D. C., in 1902.

ALBERT L. WAITERS,
1311 Gregg street, Columbia, S. C.; Headwaiter, Kenilworth Inn
Biltmore, N. C.

ALBERT L. WAITERS.

Albert L. Waiters was born on the 6th day of April, 1861, in Columbia, S. C. He commenced his hotel career as early as 1873, serving his apprenticeship in the Washington House and Columbia Hotel of his native city. He early showed his fitness to assume responsibility and to command men, and was given charge of the "Percell" at Wilmington, N. C., serving successfully during the season of 1879. From there he was called to the Florida House at St. Augustine, Fla., finishing the season with credit and honor to himself and the house. He thence went to the Central Hotel at Spartansburg, S. C., where he remained until April, 1880.

The following season, at the earnest solicitation of friends, Mr. Waiters was persuaded to accept a flattering offer to go to Sulphur Springs, N. C., in the capacity of chef. Leaving there at the close of the season, he took charge successively, and until 1891, of the Oakland Inn, the Swannanoa, and the Wynyah Sanitorium, all of Asheville, N. C. He then was given *carte blanche* in the engagement of a crew of 51 men for the famous Kenilworth Inn. Remaining at this place until 1897, he entered the service of the Florida East Coast System as head waiter for the Key West Hotel, Key West. At the close of the season he took charge of Lookout Inn, Chattanooga, Tenn.; and after one of the most successful seasons ever known at this hostelry, he returned to superintend the dining room of the Kenilworth. At the close of his engagement at the Kenilworth, Mr. Waiters was offered the Lake Harbor Hotel, that pleasant summer resort which overlooks Lake Michigan and which is made doubly more pleasant by the cool breezes which sweep over that great inland sea. Winding up a season here, which will always be remembered as one of the most pleasant and successful ones in his career, he returned to the Kenilworth and remained there until he was called to the New Gladstone, at Narragansett Pier, R. I.

His is truly a remarkable record. Some persons believe in luck and if Mr. Waiters is lucky because he fell in the right groove and by strict attention to duty and with laudable ambition, improved his condition at every step, then it would be well for everyone who wishes to succeed in life to copy from his example if they want to have some luck fall their way.

Mr. Waiters is rewarded for his efficient services by having at the present time the responsible positions of the dining room department of the Kenilworth, Asheville, N. C., and the New Gladstone at Narragansett Pier, R. I.—winter and summer resorts. The management of these houses has unlimited confidence in his ability, for his wide experience entitles him to be an authority on all matters concerning hotel and catering work. If all the colored men in hotel life were men like Mr. Waiters, there is no hesitation in saying that instead of seeing the colored waiter debarred from the best houses in eastern cities, it would be just the opposite—they would be sought after.

Long, and in increased numbers may men of his type grace the calling and raise still higher the standard of intelligence and efficiency in dining room waiting.

L. D. HOUSTON.

L. D. Houston was born in Salisbury, Md., sixty years ago. When a boy, he was sent to New Orleans and served on the Mississippi River steamers. After enduring for seven years the cruel treatment of those dark days in which man's inhumanity to man was manifested at its severest, his young spirit rebelled and sought refuge in escape, which he made to Vera Cruz, Mexico. Arriving there, free from the cage of bondage, and the fire of ambition to succeed being kindled in him, he soon found things too slow, as is the case is most tropical countries; he, therefore, shipped on a German vessel going to Europe. From London, he went around the Horn to California, and from there to Hong Kong, China, where he made his home for seven years. Some of the best days of Mr. Houston's life were spent in this Eastern country. While in China, he was employed as steward on many of the boats running up the great rivers of that country.

When in a reminiscent mood, he often relates his experience in China. The inferences drawn from a recital of these reminiscences show that his days spent in China were very happy ones, and that during that period, had the young man possessed the wisdom in true economy, as has been developed since, he would have been a wealthy man to-day. But, naturally, youth is almost always mistaken as to a constant flow of the stream of health, wealth and vigor. However, Mr. Houston did not long chase the rainbow, and to-day, though not a wealthy man, is healthy and vigorous, and financially, is one of the foundation stones on which the race's structure will rest.

At the end of the Civil War in 1867, longing for the land of his nativity, he came to America, and settled down in New York, where he has remained ever since. Soon after his arrival he entered the hotel occupation, going to the summer resorts during the summer seasons, and carrying on a catering business during the winter months. He is one of the oldest head waiters in the business. Since 1874 he has had charge of fourteen different hotels, and has always been successful in closing the seasons with satisfaction to his employers and with credit to himself.

No head waiter is better known to the struggling young man than is Mr. Houston. He is known to be the good fairy to many of the young men who are pursuing their studies at college, and work during the summer months for enough money to carry them through

L. D. HOUSTON.

Headwaiter St. James' Hotel, New York City, and Peninsula Hotel, Seabright, N. J.

the next term. To these young men he always gives first consideration; but Howard University young men are his favorites and, to them he gives the preference. Many a man who is to-day earning his living in the profession as minister, teacher, lawyer, and doctor, has found employment with Mr. Houston. He is in charge of the Peninsula Hotel, Seabright, N. J., where he has been for the last fifteen seasons. During the winter, he is in charge of the dining room of the St. James' Hotel, New York, under the same proprietor at a salary of $900 per annum.

Mr. Houston is known among the young men as "Old man Houston" and takes a delight in being so called. His brother, Mr. S. T. Houston, of Salisbury, Md., is one of the best known men in the State. He retired from the hotel business some years ago on his well deserved laurels, and is now enjoying the eventide of his life in quietness and contentment, living on the income of his earnings, which, in his early years of activity, he had so prudently saved.

Mr. L. D. Houston is very spry for his age, and anyone who does not know him, would take him to be a man of about forty years of age. The secret of his youth is his love and enjoyment of the companionship of young people. He believes in only looking as old as he feels. The only thing that gives his age away, is when he is quizzed about getting married (for he is a confirmed bachelor), then he will say, "I never intend to get married, for it is too late now." May Mr. Houston and the men of his stamp, remain with us a long time.

Mr. Houston is a member of the Head, Second and Side Waiters National Benefit Association.

J. F. GILBERT.
Headwaiter The Andersen Hotel, Pittsburg, Pa.

JOHN T. GILBERT.

John T. Gilbert has been at the Hotel Anderson, Pittsburg, Pa., for nineteen and a half years, as head waiter. When he came to this house from the famous "Neil House," Columbus, Ohio, it was predicted that he would not remain in the position for two months, because seven head waiters had been previously discharged in as many years.

To quote Mr. Gilbert's own words would best convey the character of the man, for there is nothing that can be said that could give as fair an idea of the reasons for his success as his own account of his deep religious convictions. He says: "I cannot and will not attempt to give a sketch of my hotel career without first thanking the commanding Chief of us all for the success which has attended me in the past years. It is to him and to him alone that success comes who obeys the Divine will of the One who rules heaven and earth. I do not believe that any man can be successful and happy who leaves the great Commander out of his calculations. As an instance, there was that great martyr, William McKinley, who was endowed with all the gifts that nature could bestow on man and the love of a great nation, but he was so prudent and mindful of his obligations to his Creator that he dared not take up the reins of government before consecrating his life to God. And what was the result? Happiness and prosperity throughout the land.

"Just so it was with myself when I took charge of the dining room. I secured the very best help I could find, men with strict moral characters and religious tendencies and the result has been all that a man can desire, for I have unlimited confidence in my men and they have the same in me. We are a unit in the conscientious discharge of our duties, for we are actuated by something higher than selfish motives.

"I have now been in the employ of the present firm of Henry and T. T. McKinnie at the Hotel Anderson, one of the best known commercial hotels in the United States, for nineteen and a half years. I have never been absent from my business for one week and will give one hundred dollars in gold to anyone who will prove that I have ever been docked one dollar since I have been in the employ of this firm.

It was prophesied that I would not retain my position for two months, but I am still at my post.

"I own the house I live in, 72 Congress street and Fifth avenue, Pittsburg, and am interested in property on Mt. Vernon and St. Clair avenues, Columbus, Ohio, my former home; also in Urbana, Ohio. God has been my captain and I beseech my fellow head waiters to devote themselves absolutely to the cultivation of those principles which will give the most happiness in this life and the life to come, and which cannot fail to attract to them the confidence and respect of their employers and the fidelity of the men who serve under them."

JOHN C. LOGAN.

John C. Logan, superintendent of the dining room of the Portland Hotel, Portland, Ore., was born in the year 1860, in Columbia, S. C. At the age of fifteen he went to New York City, where he received his first introduction in the service of waiting on the Steamer Thomas Powell, then plying between New York City and Troy. On leaving this boat, in 1876, he went to the Cosmopolitan Hotel, New York City, under head waiter Mr. William Brown. After a period of service in this hotel he left and for a number of years during the summer seasons went to Shelter Island, L. I., and at other times to Long Branch, New Jersey, and in the winter season to Jacksonville or St. Augustine, Fla., where he waited in some of the leading hotels in these places.

In the year 1886 Mr. Logan had his first experience as a high officer in the dining room. He was first assistant head waiter to Mr. Glover, of pleasant memory, at the Battery Park Hotel, Asheville, N. C. Mr. Glover was then considered one of the best head waiters in America and was selected by Colonel Cox, of Philadelphia, to take charge of the dining room of this palatial hotel, with a crew selected in New York. It therefore speaks well for Mr. Logan that he was selected in preference to many other applicants for the position, as second in command to Mr. Glover; and it evidenced his fitness for the place, that upon the resignation of Mr. Glover, six months later, he was given the full charge of the dining room without his asking for the promotion, and, in fact, against his wishes, as he felt, though quite competent, that he was too young to shoulder the responsibility of the office and the commanding of so large a number of men. However, Mr. Chas. H. Southwick, the manager, would not countenance his refusal; therefore Mr. Logan submitted to his desire and proved that the confidence which his employers had in his abilities was well founded by his holding the position for two years. At the end of this period he was obliged to resign on account of ill health and to go to the White Sulphur Springs, N. C.

On recovery from his illness, in 1900, he accepted under contract for one year the position of assistant head waiter to the late Mr. Thomas H. Frazier, who was engaged to take charge and open the Portland Hotel, Portland, Ore., then being opened for the first time.

JOHN C. LOGAN.
Headwaiter, Portland Hotel, Portland, Ore.

Before the expiration of his term at the Portland he was engaged to superintend the dining room of the Spokane Hotel, Spokane, Wash. He was at this hotel three months when Mr. Frazier resigned from the Portland, the management of which immediately requested Mr. Logan to return and take full charge. He therefore resigned from the Spokane and returned to the Portland, where he still remains as the commander of its dining room.

It was good fortune for Mr. Logan to have received his early training in the calling from such proficient men of the old school as Messrs. Brown, Glover and Frazier.

He is up-to-date in everything that appertains to the dining room, and is at all time equipoised and tranquil in the performance of his duties, with a profusion of courtesy for every one. Tall and erect, like a cavalier, and with the dignity of a European Prime Minister, he receives the guests as they enter to enjoy the luxurious repast of that great hotel of the far Northwest.

Mr. Logan makes it one of his principal duties to train every man under him up to the highest degree of efficiency. He is a member of the Head, Second and Side Waiters' National Benefit Association.

SAMUEL R. WILSON.
Headwaiter Hotel Oglethorpe, Brunswick, Ga.

SAM RANDLE WILSON.

Sam Randle Wilson, the subject of this sketch, is at present head waiter of the Hotel Oglethorpe, Brunswick, Ga. Mr. Wilson was born on the 7th of May, 1870, at La Grange, Ga. His rapid rise to the top of his calling, and to the management of the dining room of one of the leading houses in the South, is the best recommendation that can be given of his abilities; for it must be remembered that hotel proprietors and managers are men of keen perception, and are on the lookout for capable men only to place at the head of that department which is the lode-stone of all hotels—the dining room.

Mr. Wilson commenced his vocation at the La Grange Hotel in his native city, at the age of fourteen. In 1887 he went to the Clifford House, Birmingham, Ala., and in 1889 to the Reade House, Chattanooga, Tenn. During the same year he acted as third man at the Louisville Hotel, Louisville, Ky., and in the following year as second man at the Burnett House, Cincinnati, Ohio. After this, he went to the Kimball House, thence to the Aragon, where he remained for several years as chief in the café.

In 1896 he went to the Central Hotel, Charlotte, N. C., as head waiter, and then back to the Kimball House café, where he remained until 1899, when he took charge of the Oglethorpe—the finest hotel in Georgia, and the one that handles the best trade of the South. This hotel accommodates the wealthy tourists who arrive in Brunswick, coming from the North, East and West, going to Jekyll Island.

Mr. Wilson is one of the prominent members connected with the Head, Second and Side Waiters' National Benefit Association, and his counsel in the deliberations during the conventions of the Association is always listened to with marked respect. Though quite a young man, he has very progressive ideas, and possesses an amount of experience and ability far beyond his years; there is, therefore, no doubt that as the years roll on, Mr. Wilson will continue to forge ahead until he reaches that point where he will receive that recognition which will place him among the foremost of his race; for in him are found in a very large measure, all the elements that contribute to material success.

As men of Mr. Wilson's type continue to increase, the greater will be the predominating influences which will control and shape the future destiny of his race.

CHARLES T. FERGUSON,

Headwaiter Strand Hotel, Atlantic City, N. J.; Member of Board of Management, H., S. & S. W. N. B. Assn.

CHARLES THOMAS FERGUSON.

The subject of this sketch, Charles Thomas Ferguson, is head of the dining room department of one of the leading hotels in Atlantic City, N. J., "The Paradise of American summer resorts," and is one of the leading dining-room superintendents on the American continent.

Mr. Ferguson was born in Virginia, on October 2nd, 1860. He began life as a farm boy while attending the public school. After securing a fair education at the Hampton Institute, Hampton, Va., he secured a teacher's position, and taught school for three years, at the end of which time he abandoned this calling.

He commenced his career as a waiter in a hash house in the city of Washington, D. C. After serving in many of the leading hotels in Washington, he secured employment at the White House, as chief butler to the late Benjamin Harrison, then President of the United States, at a very good salary. Near the close of Mr. Harrison's administration, Mr. Ferguson was transferred to one of the departments as a promotion for the excellent service he had rendered as butler. Eight months later, however, owing to a political transformation, President Cleveland, who succeeded Mr. Harrison, gave Mr. Ferguson an indefinite vacation. Soon after leaving the department, he secured a position as head waiter at the Willard House, Washington, at which place he added much to his reputation as a man of great ability. His established reputation has caused his services to be very much sought after by managers of many leading hotels throughout the country, and he has ever since been employed in some one of the leading hotels, giving perfect satisfaction, and remaining for the full term of his contract.

Mr. Ferguson always employs a first-class crew of men. He keeps them under perfect control, and maintains the best of discipline. He is a tireless worker, and observes keenly every minute detail, allowing no work, however insignificant, to pass without his inspection. His motto is "Economy of time, and thorough performance of duty." He is at present the head waiter of the Hotel Strand, one of the leading hotels in Atlantic City, N. J., at which hotel he has been head of the dining-room department for the past three years.

Mr. Ferguson apparently intends to make Atlantic City his future home, as he has bought a very fine residence at the corner of Arctic and Indiana streets.

He is a member of the Head, Second and Side Waiters' National Benefit Association, and also a member of the Board of Managers. Mr. Ferguson is tall, erect and quite polished in his manners, and is exceedingly agreeable.

THOMAS A. WOOD.

Thomas A. Wood was born at Statesville, Iredell County, N. C., October 22nd, 1864.

He is known to the hotel world as a man who is thoroughly acquainted with all that pertains to the hotel dining room, and the service and efficiency of the men needed to make a dining room all that it should be.

He was one of eight children, and early in life was thrown on his own resources to maintain himself, and to assist his stricken mother who was deprived of the support of her husband (his father) by death. Little, therefore, can be said of his early school life, but, brief as it was, Mr. Wood never forgot a motto he read while pounding over the three R's, viz.: "Aim high." It is Emerson's admonition to young men about chaining their ambition to the chariot of the sun. His thirst for knowledge has been insatiable, and although unable to acquire it in his youth, he has nevertheless in his years of maturity made up for lost time by burning the midnight oil. He maintains that knowledge gained and properly applied, is the royal road that leads to perfect happiness, and that the cultivation of mind is the culmination of man's desire. Mr. Wood believes also that, the more developed the mind and the higher the man progresses in the truths which comprise the science of the spiritual and physical life, the nearer is that man to his God. As he himself puts it: "The Fates seeing my unswerving perseverance to be somebody in life, pitied me and taught me other lessons than those learned in school."

At the age of sixteen Mr. Wood commenced his hotel life as a side waiter, at the St. Charles Hotel in his native town. This was followed by his having the same position at the Swannanoa, in the center of the highlands of North Carolina. His next step was one of more importance, for he became second waiter under John Glascow, at the Battery Park Hotel, Asheville, N. C., the Italy of America.

It is interesting to know that the spot on which this hotel stands was once a fortress, garrisoned by Confederate soldiers. In this there is a moral; for on that site of a once fortress, commanded by Captains who dealt out death to strangers and hated the Northern men, there now stands an imposing edifice reared to peace, where Captains of

THOMAS A. WOOD.
Headwaiter The Hathaway Inn, Deal Beach, N. J.

the dining room like Mr. Wood, deal out healthy viands to visitors, and welcome the Northern man; where merry laughter is now heard instead of groans and curses; where the only explosion is from the popping of corks in the exchange of friendly greetings, instead of the bursting of shell and the discharge of cannon in the desire of angry men to destroy their brethren. And may this latter scene never be changed. During the year 1893 Mr. Wood served as second waiter to Mr. Thomas J. Simons, of the Michigan Columbian Club, at the World's Fair, Chicago.

After this, he became imbued with the desire to pursue his calling in a house of greater repute, and one in which he could gain further knowledge, and so accepted a place at the Hotel Champlain, N. Y., as second waiter under Mr. Frank P. Thompson. The following year, owing to ill health, Mr. Wood was unable to accept any position, and so remained at his home in North Carolina, recuperating among the hills.

In 1901, however, he accepted the position of head waiter at the Battery Park Hotel, Asheville, N C., and in the following year took charge of the dining room of the famous summer resort on the Jersey Coast, The Hathaway Inn.

The winter of 1903 again found him with Mr. Frank P. Thompson as second man at the Ponce de Leon, St. Augustine, Fla., and during the summer just past, 1903, he served his second season at the Hathaway Inn, New Jersey.

Mr. Wood is a man of fine physique, well proportioned, dignified in his bearing, and is indeed the ideal head waiter. It is his pride that such rules and regulations as he lays down for the guidance of his men, have been conducive of the very best results, and many of them are original.

While Mr. Wood requires from his men the highest efficiency in their individual service, it cannot be said of him that he is exacting or arbitrary. He is loved by them, and is always mindful of their interests. He is also one of the leading members of the Head, Second and Side Waiters' National Benefit Association, and one of the men in the calling who have made provision for a rainy day.

C. B. COLES.
Headwaiter Yale University Dining Rooms, New Haven. Conn.

C. B. COLES.

C. B. Coles, head waiter at Yale University, New Haven, Conn., was born in Virginia, on February 18th, 1866.

After working on his father's farm until he was thirteen years of age, he went to work for a party who was surveying the route of the Shenandoah Valley Railroad. At the completion of this work, he secured a job as driver on one of the carts for this same road. Having at the end of six months proven his efficiency, he was paid the same wages as the other men received. When the road was finally completed, he was made a section laborer. His tact and intelligence soon earned him promotion to the foremanship of his gang.

Becoming tired of this life, however, he secured employment at the well-known Hine Furnace, which is located at Clifton Forge, Va. After 18 months of service there, he paid a visit to his parents. While on his visit, he met one of the officials of the Shenandoah Railroad, who offered him a position as flagman on the road, at which occupation he remained until he was stricken with typhoid pneumonia, an illness, that incapacitated him for two years. On his recovery, however, his strength having been greatly impaired, he felt himself no longer able to undertake any heavy manual labor. Thinking that hotel life would best suit him, he went to National Bridge, Va., and secured a place as waiter in the Forest Inn. It was at this place that his career as a waiter began. After remaining there for six months, he paid another visit to his aged parents, and while there, concluded to try Washington City; he secured employment, but needing more experience for the service in such grand hotels, he did not at first succeed. After many months he secured a place in a German family as useful man; and at the expiration of one year he was fortunate enough to obtain a job in the National Hotel, where he remained four years.

In the year 1887, he worked in the Octagon Hotel, Seabright, N. J. At the end of the season he returned to Washington, but finding no employment, went to New London, Conn., and found work in the Pequot House. At this place his bearing and worth made such a favorable impression on one of the guests, Mr. Silvanus Reed, of 6 West 53rd street, New York City, that he engaged him as butler, where he remained that winter. During the summer of 1889, Mr. Coles worked at the Grand Union Hotel, Saratoga, Springs, N. Y.

At the end of that season the love of parents and home, again took him to Virginia. After a happy reunion, he again essayed Washington, the Nation's capitol; but soon after made his way to New York City, and was engaged as butler by Mr. G. W. Eley, of the New York Stock Exchange. On leaving his service later, he went to work at the Lotis Club, 5th avenue and 46th street.

From there Mr. Coles took service in the Sherman Square Hotel, Boulevard and 71st street, New York City. Working there for seven years, he filled every place in the hotel dining room except head waiter, although he acted in that capacity during the summer months, while the head waiter, Mr. Randolph, was at summer resorts.

At the expiration of that term Mr. Coles was fortunate enough to secure the position of head waiter of the dining room of the Colorado Hotel, Belmar, N. J. Here his intelligent and faithful service made such an excellent impression on the hotel manager that, in the spring of 1900, he was placed in charge of the dining rooms of the Hotel Endicott, one of the most exclusive in the country, situated at Columbus avenue and 81st street, New York City, where he remained until late in the autumn of the same year. In the spring of 1901, the same manager sent for him to resume his former position as head waiter. There he remained until the close of the hotel for repairs in the summer.

Shortly afterwards, Mr. Coles succeeded a white head waiter in the Victoria Hotel, Larchmont, N. Y.

While at the latter hotel he was called to open and take charge of the Yale University dining hall, at which time preparations were being made for the great bi-centennial celebration in the autumn of 1901.

There Mr. Coles' ability as a first-class head waiter was demonstrated in successfully commanding 210 waiters and serving 2,600 guests at each meal, during that long and trying session of the celebration.

In June, 1902, Mr. Coles served a banquet numbering between 1,600 and 1,800 guests. On this occasion, he was paid many compliments, on his management of affairs. The chief manager was so much pleased with his work that he then and there engaged him for the function of the following season.

During the summer months of 1902, Mr. Coles engaged as second head waiter at the new Grand Hotel, Catskill Mountains, N. Y. On account of illness in the family of the head waiter, he was placed in charge to close the season. At the close of the season he returned to the Yale University dining room, where he is still head waiter, and giving the most efficient service as a dining room superintendent. Mr. Coles is a member of the Head, Second and Side Waiters' National Benefit Association. He is considered one of the most efficient head waiters in this country. He is exceedingly ambitious, possesses much race pride, and is a proficient educator in all that pertains to the hotel dining room. He is connected with many of the leading negro enterprises of to-day.

HARVEY C. GREEN, Clayville, Va.
Headwaiter Royal Palace, Atlantic City, N. J.

HARVEY CARLISLE GREEN.

The subject of this sketch was born in Petersburg, Va., December 14th, 1865. Having received a thorough education in the Public Schools of his home, he was graduated with high honors.

When still a young man, Mr. Green came North and located in New Jersey, where he speedily secured a position as butler in one of the oldest and most aristocratic families of the State. He served in this family for a number of years, gaining an enviable prestige on account of his gentlemanly bearing, and sterling qualities.

Having a desire to widen his scope of activity, Mr. Green accepted a position as third head waiter at the Burnett House, Cincinnati, Ohio, where after a short period he was rapidly advanced by his superior, Mr. Wm. T. Green. Leaving there he went to the Mitchell House, in Thomasville, Ga., where he was elevated to the position of second head waiter, a position which he filled from 1886 to 1889, and served during the winter seasons as head waiter.

In 1889 he accepted the position of head waiter at the new American Hotel, Richfield Springs, N. Y., where he remained for three seasons. From this place he went during the summer months to the New Cliff Hotel, Newport, R. I.

During the winter months of '98 and '99 Mr. Green went to St. Augustine, Fla., and served as second waiter under Mr. Frank P. Thompson at the Ponce de Leon. Mr. Green also spent two winter seasons at the Hotel Ormond, Ormond, Fla., and he has the distinction of being the first colored head waiter to serve at this place. The winter of 1902 found Mr. Green at the Royal Palm, Miami, Fla.

During his many years of service Mr. Green has enjoyed the confidence of his employers and is loved and esteemed highly by his men.

It is perhaps due to the fact that Mr. Green carries with him at all times a class of men of the highest efficiency in their calling, that he has been able to attain such high standing as a head waiter; in fact it is commonly acknowledged that his men are among the very best waiters to be found anywhere.

Mr. Green speaks in the highest terms of his second and third waiters and also of his secretary, and says that their unsullied reputation has been such as not only to reflect credit to themselves, but to him as well, and he thinks he has cause to be proud of them.

As a head waiter Mr. Green is noted for his politeness and gentlemanly bearing. He possesses a polish of manners that is indeed enviable, and is in his second season at the Royal Palace, Atlantic City, N. J.

CHARLES S. SMITH.
Headwaiter, Belgravia, Philadelphia, Pa.

CHARLES S. SMITH.

Charles S. Smith was born in Williamburg, Va., on December 20th, 1870. His father and mother died before he had entered his teens, so that his earlier days were not strewn with roses. His position to-day, among those in the front rank in his calling, is principally due to his untiring energy, force of character and a zealous desire for success.

Mr. Smith attributes his success to the determination which he made when he commenced his career, to perform his duties in as thorough and as perfect a manner as it was possible for him to do, and his success in later life ought to be an encouragement to young men to pursue the path of rectitude, and to be courteous and obliging in their intercourse with their fellow men at all times.

Mr. Smith's first experience in hotel life was at the Hygeia Hotel, Old Point Comfort, Va., in 1888, where he served for two seasons. In 1890 he went to Washington, D. C., and secured a position at the Spanish Legation as messenger. In 1894 he went to Philadelphia, and secured a position as second waiter at the Bingham House, where he remained for two years. On leaving there he went to Atlantic City and there took charge of the Glaslyn Hotel, for the season of 1896. The following season found him in charge of the Holmeshurst, at Atlantic City, and in 1898 he returned to Philadelphia, to take charge of the Ridgway House for three seasons. During the next three seasons he had charge of the Hotel Lafayette, Cape May, N. J., one of the largest and best equipped hotels on the Atlantic Coast. Since then he has been in charge of the Irving House, Philadelphia, one of the oldest and most exclusive hostelries in the Quaker City.

Wherever Mr. Smith happens to be his pleasing manners are sure to gain for him the esteem of his employer as well as the guests of the house. His business-like way of conducting his department, must be seen to be fully appreciated, for his system of doing things, and his entire mastery of details are gifts amounting to genius. His friends are legion, and they always have a kind word to say for him.

The loss of Mr. Smith's parents so early in life, deprived him of the opportunities in youth to enrich his natural ability. Be this as it may, however, he now makes up for this loss as he continues his journey through life, for he loses no opportunity to educate himself in the world's university of general affairs. And thus it is that every day's sun sets upon a mind on which some good impression has been made, some lesson from experience learnt, and each morning dawns upon a mind expanded and made more fruitful by the nourishment which it has received.

Unassumingly, he struggles on in the rugged path of life; step by step he moves along daily to the celestial city of perfect intellectuality, storing, as he goes, those things which make for material success.

Mr. Smith is a member of the Head, Second and Side Waiters' National Benefit Association, and one of its staunch supporters.

At the beginning of 1904 he took charge of the Hotel Belgravia, one of the finest Apartment Hotels in the city of Philadelphia.

WILLIAM E. TUCKER.

William E. Tucker, head waiter of the Albion Hotel, Augusta, Ga., is a young man whose record sheds lustre on the profession. He was born in West Point, Ga., on the 20th day of December, 1876. His size and height make him the ideal superintendent of the dining room, for he stands six feet three inches in height and weighs 175 pounds. His imposing stature and dignified bearing come as near perfection and in harmony with his calling as if these qualities were made to order.

Mr. Tucker commenced and learned his business from the bottom, for he started as a dish washer in a restaurant in West Point, Ga., conducted by Mr. W. G. Schaefer, but was soon promoted to a waiter's position.

Some of Mr. Tucker's engagements have been: Captain of silver watch, Hotel Aragon, Atlanta, Ga.; captain of day watch, Tate Springs, Tenn.; captain of day watch, Morris Hotel (European plan), Birmingham, Ala.; captain of day watch for three successive winter seasons at Bonair Hotel, Augusta, Ga.

In 1897 Mr. Tucker became head waiter of the Arlington Hotel, Gainesville, Ga.; in the summer season of 1898 he acted in the same capacity at the Park Hotel, of Gainesville, after which he went to the Bonair Hotel, Atlanta, Ga. In the summer of 1899 he went to the Tate Springs, Tennessee, as second waiter, and in July of that summer took the place of head waiter, succeeding T. J. Simon, who resigned. At the close of this season Mr. Tucker was the recipient of many testimonials from the guests and proprietors who appreciated the able manner in which he had conducted his department, and which added much to the success of the house and to the comfort of the guests. In the summer of 1900 Mr. Tucker went to the Larkin House, Watch Hill, R. I., as second waiter, and from 1901 to 1902 he was head waiter of the New Albion Hotel, Augusta, Ga. From October, 1902, to March, 1903, he was second waiter of the Chittenden Hotel, Columbus, Ohio, and in April, 1903, he was re-engaged as head waiter of the Albion, Augusta, Ga., which position he now holds.

Mr. Tucker's motto is thoroughness in everything that he does and he believes that whatever a man does should be done to the best of his ability. He has contributed a series of articles to the journal "Hotel Life," published in Cleveland, Ohio. Some of the subjects are:

WILLIAM E. TUCKER,
Headwaiter, Albion Hotel, Augusta, Ga.

"Technology on arrangements and service for special occasions"; "Correct service in the commercial hotel"; "The art in private waiting." He is known as a prolific and interesting writer. He has also contributed to such monthly periodicals as "The Hotel World," "Hotel Gazette" and "The Caterer." Extracts from his many good lectures on different occasions to the colored waiters can be found in the columns of the "Freeman" of Indianapolis for the past four years.

Every hotel proprietor who has been fortunate to employ Mr. Tucker at any time bears testimony to his energy, efficiency and progressiveness. The men who serve in a subordinate position under him, love and respect him, for he looks after their interests and protects them in their rights. In fact, Mr. Tucker is one of those object lessons of a man casting lustre on the vocation which he has chosen for a living by bringing to his aid the highest intelligence, zeal, capacity and manhood.

He is an honored member of the Head, Second and Side Waiters' National Benefit Association; and was elected vice-president for his native State, Georgia, at the convention held in Buffalo in 1901 and has been re-elected at every convention since. In this position he has always thrown his influence on the side of any measure that tends to improve the condition not only of the Head and Second Waiters, but of the side men whose interests are very near his heart.

A bright future yet awaits him and in him might arise a star whose brilliant illumination will no doubt lead, not only those in his calling, but the people with whom he is identified, to grander and greater material success.

T. C. SMITH,
Headwaiter, Macon, Ga.

THOMAS C. SMITH.

Man is a social and progressive being. Each step he takes is an inclination to higher and higher climb.

In the State of Georgia which contains the largest population of negroes in the United States, and in which they are among the most progressive in the accumulation of wealth and education, Thomas C. Smith was born, in the county of Cranford, October 11th, 1858; a period just prior to the time when the sun of liberty had burst forth in its effulgency, and shed its inspiring rays upon the darkness of millions of God's created human souls, revivifying them into the life which the creator intended that all men should live. Naturally, nothing of very great interest can be chronicled here of the early days of Mr. Smith. Like a little plant that had burst its earthen bond, and shot forth its head toward heaven after winter's frost had passed away, and struggling to catch a ray of sunshine and drops of dew or rain to brighten and elevate it, so did young Smith. Moving along from period to period, patiently plodding away, ever onward, ever upward to a higher and better day, counting each moment which was not occupied in the performance of some duty, a loss.

In the year 1878, he commenced his hotel career as a waiter in the Kimbal House, Atlanta, Ga. Two years later he went to the Metropolitan Hotel, Washington, D. C., which was under the same management; there he remained for about four years during the winter seasons, and going to the Howland House, Long Branch, N. J., during the summer seasons.

Mr. Smith has served in some of the leading houses in New York City, such as French's in Park Place, Earl's Hotel, The Rossmore, and the Old Stuyvesant in Broadway.

As a side waiter, he always gained the confidence of his commanders and the managers of the hotel, by his obedience, uprightness, strict attention to duty, and his aptness in the performance of the same, and was also a great favorite with the patrons because of his politeness and willingness to please, and to do any favor requested of him, whether he received compensation or not. For these reasons Mr. Smith found no difficulty in always securing and keeping places in the best houses, and under the most exacting head waiter.

Among the men under whom he has served are, Wilson Percival, Frank P. Thompson, Frank King, Edward Irving and W. H. Austin. After going through the various grades in his calling, Mr. Smith reached the place he had labored for. In the summer of 1886 he obtained the position of head waiter of the Mizzen Top Hotel, Pawling, N. Y. He remained in this position for ten summers, after which he made a change. He has since had charge of the Putnam, Pulaski, Fla. After that, he entered the service of the Florida East Coast, and remained with it until Mr. Knott retired from the management. He was two winters in charge of the Cardoza, St. Augustine, Fla., after which he was assigned to the Alcazar, St. Augustine, from which he was transferred to the Royal Poinciana, Palm Beach, and to which place he took the first crew of colored waiters that succeeded the white. The following season, he was sent to the Royal Palm, Miami, Fla. At this house he held the charge for five winters. He has also had charge of the Monmouth House, N. J., and the Pequot, New London, for several seasons.

Mr. Smith stands high in the rank of that class of negro headwaiters in the country whose places when they shall have passed away, will be hard to fill, and whose successful career has been linked with the progressive development of the hotel business.

Man being a social as well as a progressive being, though he may neglect the social side while struggling for that success which brings material benefit, as soon as he obtains a fair measure of it, his bosom heaves for the solace and the refining influence of society, and he therefore seeks for it in a life companion. Thus it was that in May, 1895, Mr. Smith took unto himself a wife in the person of Miss Carrie Dishroom. They have since been blessed with the bright prattle of T. C. Smith, Jr.

Mr. Smith is undoubtedly a born leader of men. For a man in his calling he possesses marked ability. As a commander he controls his men with firmness and rigid justice, yet tempered with the sweetest of human kindness. His judgment is clear. Unswerving honesty and unvarying politeness with and to all, are two of the principal elements to his success, and those qualities he always impresses upon his men. He is therefore highly appreciated by them as well as the hotel management, patrons, and the general public. He is one of the men in the calling who, in the days of sunshine, think of the clouds and the rain that to-morrow might bring forth, and has, therefore, made provision for the possible exigencies of such days. He caters always for the best houses, and endeavors to give an ideal service. His motto for success is obedience and conscientious labor. He makes it his duty on every possible occasion to instil in the minds of his men the advantage of good society, and the cultivation of business habits and thrift, and teaches by practice the principle of true economy, the strict practice of which is so very necessary to the progress of his race, but which nevertheless is practiced by it, as a rule, more in the breach than in the observance. Such men as Mr. Smith are of the material out of which the foundation stone of the structure of the future race is made.

JOHN T. STANTON,
Headwaiter, Pittsburg, Pa.

JOHN T. STANTON.

John T. Stanton was born on the 26th day of March, 1863, in Carlisle, Cumberland County, Pa. He went to school in his native city, where the influence of those good people who belong to the Quaker faith had a marked influence on his life. He commenced his career in a private family at the age of fifteen. In 1880, at the age of seventeen, he went to Mansfield, Ohio, and served for one year under head waiter Blair Dunmore, at the St. James' Hotel; the two following years he worked in Indianapolis, under head waiter John Steward, at the Bates House. Leaving there in 1883, he went to Chicago and served under head waiter Charles Lewis, and in 1884 he went to the Grand Pacific Hotel, Chicago, under head waiter Wm. Murry; from there to the Palmer House under head waiter Charles Jordan for three years. In 1888 he left for Cleveland, Ohio, and secured employment under Ralph Williams, at the Forest City House; thence to the Hotel Anderson, Pittsburg, Pa., in 1890, under head waiter John Nixon.

Moving stey by step up the ladder, he became in 1891 the second head waiter at the Weddell House, Cleveland, O., and two years after took charge as head waiter of the Wilmont Hotel, Cleveland, O., where he remained for many years, making a change afterwards to the Hotel Gettysburg, Gettysburg, Pa. In the summer seasons of 1898 and 1899, he was employed respectively as second waiter at the Scarboro Hotel, Long Branch, N. J., and at the Grand Union, Saratoga Springs. Not having any official charge in 1900 Mr. Stanton worked as a side waiter at the Lochiel Hotel, Harrisburg, and in 1902 he was promoted to the head waiter's position, which place he held until recently.

A record like this is truly praiseworthy, and is a fair example of the perseverance necessary to success in the struggle for subsistence.

The varied experience of Mr. Stanton is something that money cannot buy—it must be gone through step by step to be appreciated. It gives the possessor an insight into human nature and the varied customs of the country, which insight is useful to a head waiter in the handling of the patrons who visit his dining rooms. Mr. Stanton can tell at a glance the peculiar idiosyncracies of a guest and handle him accordingly—one of the faculties every head waiter should possess to be successful.

Mr. Stanton is a member of the Head, Second and Side Waiters' National Benefit Association, and a warm advocate of everything that the Association is doing to better the condition and advance the mutual interest of employers and employees.

He is a very progressive young man and believes that no hill is too rugged to climb, if one must reach the broad plain of success above. The easy path in life is to an individual, race or nation, but a chance occurrence. It is nature's will that man should struggle hard, step by step, to gain the "Heights great men have reached and kept."

A. C. PITTS.

Mr. A. C. Pitts modestly says: "I began life as a dishwasher in a restaurant in Macon, Ga., and later worked as a side waiter in the same place.

"The first house of note in which I was employed was the Upland, in Eastman, Ga., under Mr. F. N. Schofield. From there I went to Saratoga Springs and became a side waiter in the Grand Union Hotel."

It was in 1883 that Mr. Pitts became a side waiter in the well-known Taylor House, in Jersey City, N. J. In the year 1884 he was made a private waiter in the St. Augustine House, at St. Augustine, Fla., where he was "Captain of the Watch," and in which capacity he served for three seasons. Following this he served for two seasons as "Captain of the Watch" at the famous St. James' Hotel, Jacksonville, Fla. While in this position he gave such appreciable satisfaction, that at the end of the season he was employed to serve in the Jekyll Island Club, Brunswick, Ga. From that house he went as second waiter to the Pavilion House, Staten Island, N. Y. The next season Mr. Pitts served in the Columbia Hotel, at Belmar, N. J. His first position as head waiter was at the Short Beach Club, Babylon, L. I., in the year 1889.

For six seasons Mr. Pitts served as "Captain of the Watch" in the Sherman Square Hotel, New York City, after which he became head waiter; which position he held for two more seasons. Here, as elsewhere, Mr. Pitts gave ample satisfaction to the guests as well as the management.

Later he was employed in the Century Club, of New York City. From that club, Mr. Pitts went to Boston, Mass., where he took charge of the dining room in the most popular European plan hotel in New England, the Bellview. Here, again, Mr. Pitts demonstrated his ability as an efficient head waiter. He next took charge of the dining room of the Greenwich Inn, at Sound Beach, where he remained for two years.

In an interview, Mr. Pitts thus expressed himself: "My opinion as to why the white waiter is supplanting the black, is this: Americans have the natural or rather unnatural desire to ape all the European fads, and the hotel proprietors, realizing what their patrons desire, supply the demand. But in all that goes to make up good ser-

A. C. PITTS,
Ass't. Headwaiter, Yale University Dining Hall, New Haven, Conn.

vice; neatness, quickness, courtesy, and attention to guests, the negro waiter has no superior. So the real cause of the black waiter being superseded by the white is the imitativeness of the Americans in following European customs.

"Many hotel proprietors frankly admit the truth of this assertion, and as proof positive that the colored waiter can and does give as efficient and satisfactory service as the whites, the Union League and other noted clubs, always employ colored waiters for their banquets.

"Strange to relate, the guests of the Manhasset Hotel, at Shelter Island, on one occasion, bought safety pins for the white waiters, rather than see them carry their side towels under their arms.

"Another reason why the negro waiters are being superseded by the white is that sometimes inexperienced men are made head waiters before they have a thorough knowledge of the business.

"A finished head waiter possesses a thorough knowledge of both the American and the European dining room service, and should always select at least one day each week in which to instruct his men in the art of efficient dining room service; and should a side waiter repeatedly neglect to follow out his instructions as given, he should be discharged.

"Another and very important point in my mind is that head waiters should not reprimand a side waiter in the presence of the guests, as it is very embarrassing to both.

"I must admit, that in the a-la carté service, the colored waiter is deficient. It is only in Chicago and Boston that the negro waiters are up to the standard of the highest efficiency in the a-la carté service; in these two cities they are unsurpassed."

At the Yale dining hall where Mr. Pitts is now second head waiter, there have been some very large and representative gatherings. On one occasion the waiters handled about 1,600 guests with perfect satisfaction. At the greatest of all the banquets the number of colored waiters in attendance was only 163, and yet everything passed off satisfactorily.

Mr. Pitts holds that the negro waiter works more conscientiously and more in the interest of his employers than do the waiters of any other nationality.

In the matter of dining room service, Mr. Pitts has given deep study to the calling, and, therefore, speaks with authority. He thoroughly understands the requirements as well as the innate qualifications necessary to be a good waiter, and he seeks always, to give his men the benefit of his experience. He is loved by them, and highly respected by his employers.

JAMES H. WHITEHEAD,
Headwaiter, Philadelphia, Pa.

JAMES H. WHITEHEAD.

James H. Whitehead, of whom we now write, was born in Tarboro, N. C., on the 12th day of December, in the year 1869.

His early years were spent in his native town, where he was employed at various occupations until he had become about 20 years of age.

In the year 1889, Mr. Whitehead felt that he wanted to see more of the country, and, therefore, he decided to leave Tarboro. He went to Norfolk, Va., where he afterwards found employment in the St. James' Hotel, where he remained for four years, serving most of this time as a side waiter.

The desire for travel with the hope of seeing and learning more was still exerting its influence on Mr. Whitehead, and so in 1893 he left Norfolk, and proceeded to Philadelphia, Pa. After reaching this city, his first engagement was at the Pasco Apartment Hotel, where he remained for two years, serving as a waiter. In the spring of 1895 he left this place, and was next heard from in Reading, Pa., where he became a side waiter in the Mansion House, and where he remained for a period of about eighteen months. In the year 1898 Mr. Whitehead went to Atlantic City, N. J., and there procured employment in the United States Hotel as side waiter. While at this place Mr. Whitehead's ability, respect and the conscientious discharge of his duties, made him very popular with all; he remained in the service here for two seasons.

In 1900 he went from that hotel to The Loraine, where he worked as a side waiter until the destruction of this hotel by fire the following year.

In the spring of 1902, Mr. Whitehead went to Philadelphia, and entered the catering business for himself, and he hopes to build up a large and reputable business in that city, as he is utilizing all of his ability and knowledge to this end.

Mr. Whitehead believes that patience and persistency intelligently directed, with efficient service, will ultimately bring to him merited reward, and thus repay him for his efforts.

There seems to be a bright future ahead for Mr. Whitehead, and it is hoped that his highest ambition will be fully realized.

He is a member of the Head, Second and Side Waiters' National Benefit Association.

N. C. JOHNS
Headwaiter, Empire House, Syracuse, N. Y.

NICHOLAS CHRISTOPHER JOHNS.

Nicholas Christopher Johns was born at Burrowsville, Va., and at an early age he moved to Vineland, N. J., with his parents. This was a fortunate change for Mr. Johns, for the advantages of the thorough education which he received in the public schools of his adopted city, has enabled him to fill many positions of honor and trust.

Mr. Johns' first experience in hotel service was at the old Merchants' Hotel at Cape May, N. J. He next went to the West End, 16th and Chestnut streets, Philadelphia, and remained there for nearly two years. The season of 1880, found him at the Old Ocean House, Newport, R. I. The following season, he had charge of the Trivilla Cottage, at Branchtown, Pa.; a summer resort near Philadelphia. Desirous of making a change, Mr. Johns obtained a situation in Mr. Wanamaker's store in Philadelphia and remained with this firm for five years.

In the year 1891, Mr. Johns came to New York City and obtained a position of some responsibility on the Albany day and People's line of steamers. On leaving this employ he was presented with testimonials which any man would be proud to possess. During the season of 1900, Mr. Johns was located at the Kent House, Lakewood, N. J., and was captain of the morning watch and at the close of the season he accepted the second waitership at the Reed House, Erie, Pa. He was later induced to leave this house by an offer from the proprietor of the Powers Hotel, Rochester, N. Y., to take second place at this hotel. Going to Syracuse on the termination of his employment at Rochester, Mr. Johns accepted a position at the Yates Hotel, where he remained for some time.

Mr. Johns has traveled extensively over the country as a private detective for the railroads, with headquarters at one time in Atlanta, Ga. He has been trusted in this capacity with many cases requiring the most delicate handling, combined with high intelligence, detective skill, along with much physical courage, and in such emergencies he has always given satisfaction.

Mr. Johns is a member of the National Advertising and Distributing Bureau of Chicago, and has an agency at 620 E. Washingston street, Syracuse, N. Y., and is also a member of the Head, Second and Side Waiters' National Benefit Association, in the councils of which his voice is always listened to with respect, for he is an entertaining and forceful talker.

WILLIAM A. FISHER,
Headwaiter, Atlantic Hotel, Ocean City, Md.

WILLIAM A. FISHER.

William A. Fisher was born in the city of Baltimore, Md., February 14th, 1860. He began his hotel career as a side waiter at the Bay Ridge Hotel, in the year 1886, where he served for one season. During the winter of 1886 and 1887 he waited in a restaurant, and in the spring of the latter year secured employment as a side waiter in the St. James' Hotel, Baltimore. After two months' service there, he was elevated to the position of head waiter, by reason of his ability and strict attention to business. In this capacity he served for one year. The following season he was engaged as head waiter at the Bay Ridge Hotel, where he had begun his career as a side waiter, and served for three consecutive summers. During the winter months he served as one of the leading men for Mr. James A. Harris, the most prominent caterer in Baltimore. He returned as head waiter of the St. James' in the fall of 1891, when this hotel was under the successful management of Mr. George F. Adams, who is now manager of the Chamberlain Hotel, Old Point Comfort, and he continued in this capacity for three years, when the house closed. In the fall of 1894, he went with Mr. Adams to open the Eagleton Hotel at Staunton, Va. He continued in the service of Mr. Jas. H. Harris during the winter months of the years from 1895 to 1900, and in the summer of 1901 he became head waiter of the Atlantic Hotel, Ocean City, Md., in which capacity he has served for three years. Mr. Fisher's success has been due to many commendable qualities, among which is his admirable tact in the management of the men under his control, his coolness and positiveness compels obedience, while his gentle and persuasive manner commands respect and admiration. He is the president of the Public Waiters' Association of Baltimore, one of the most influential organizations in that city. He commands the respect and admiration of all of its members.

Mr. Fisher was married in the year 1898 to Miss Lottie B. Blay, one of Baltimore's most estimable ladies, and he has a cosy little home on Presstman street. He is a member of the Head, Second and Side Waiters' National Benefit Association and was sent as a delegate to represent the Public Waiters' Association at the annual convention, held at Atlantic City, in October, 1903. He actively participated in the deliberations of the convention and succeeded in having the next convention to meet in Baltimore, in June, 1904.

A. NATHANIEL DEMPSEY,

929 Sixth avenue; Headwaiter, Hotels Flanders and Margaret, New York City, N. Y.

A. NATHANIEL DEMPSEY.

In giving a sketch of the life of Mr. A. Nathaniel Dempsey, we are fortunate in being able to place before the young men a good example of what an earnest and persevering man can accomplish. Mr. Dempsey's sole aim in view when starting out in life was to succeed—to reach the top and to keep there. What he has done, others can do. His success ought to be a beacon by which all young men who are entering on life's activities should be guided.

Mr. Dempsey was born at Hampton, Va., in the year 1860. He was brought to New York when an infant by his parents and gained his education in the Public Schools of this city.

In 1876 he entered the employ of Jones & Ryder, who were the proprietors of a restaurant at the corner of Howard street and Broadway, and later obtained employment at the St. Stephen's Hotel, West Eleventh street and Broadway.

In 1880 he secured the position of head waiter of Nut's Hotel, Nut Station, New Mexico, and remained there for two years. Wishing to branch out for himself in this new territory, he bought a large residence on the Members River, New Mexico, and converted it into a first class hotel, which he made a success of, and when a good offer was made to him to sell he readily disposed of his interest in the concern. By this time Mr. Dempsey's reputation as a hotel man was well known in this locality and he was offered the stewardship of the Exchange Club in Silver City, New Mexico. In 1885 he resigned because that longing for home which seems to overtake every American who resides for any length of time in foreign territory, made life unbearable for him. In the spring of 1886 Mr. Dempsey visited his parents in Hampton, Va., and then returned to New York. The summer of the same year he engaged as second in command of the dining room of the Prospect House, Bay Shore, L. I.

In the fall of 1886 he went to work at the Century Club, New York City, on the side, but it was not long before his abilities were recognized, and in the fall of 1887 he was promoted to the head waitership, a position he held until 1895, when he resigned and took charge of the Narrows Island Gunning Club in North Carolina. At the close of his engagement at this last place, in 1898, he was offered and accepted the head waitership of the Rodman House, Philadelphia. The summer of 1901 he went as head waiter to the Lake House, Lake George, N. Y.; and the summer of 1902, head waiter in one of the Grand Union Hotel departments, Saratoga Springs, N. Y. The summer of 1903 he took charge of the Coleman House, Atlantic City, N. J., and in the fall of the same year he opened the magnificent new apartment hotels, the Flanders and St. Margaret, New York City, where he is at present in command of the dining room.

Mr. Dempsey is a member of the Head, Second and Side Waiters' National Benefit Association, and treasurer of the local association for New York City. Such a record as Mr. Dempsey's could only have been gained by the strictest attention to duty and the exercise of abilities of no mean order when it is considered that in these days of keen competition employers are only engaging the very best men to command their dining rooms.

J. J. MILES.

J. J. Miles, head waiter of the Plankinton Hotel, Milwaukee, Wis., may well be called the nestor of the West. He was born on the 4th of July, 1845, in the grand old State of Virginia, which has furnished so many able men to the nation.

Mr. Miles' varied experience has been of great advantage to him, having traveled over two continents, Europe and America. He was engaged in various other vocations before he settled down to that which he is now making his life's calling.

In his early days as a young man he graduated from the service of the Pullman Palace Car Company which has given employment to many a young man. On leaving the Pullman service he entered that of a private club, where he remained for some time. Tiring of this work and desiring to see the world, he got an engagement which took him to Europe, over which continent he traveled for many years. He finally returned to New York City, and afterwards took a trip to San Francisco. After a while he again came East and engaged in the service of a lake steamboat.

His hotel experience has been gained in some of the largest houses in the East, such houses as the Willard, in Washington; Bramins, in Baltimore; Continental, in Philadelphia; Metropolitan, in New York City, and in many of the prominent summer resorts. He was therefore, well fitted to fill the important position he has so long filled at the Plankinton, and which could only have been filled by one of varied experience and having a keen insight into human nature, progressive and up-to-date, in fact, a broad-minded and versatile man.

Twenty-eight years ago Mr. Miles was called from the Grand Pacific Hotel in Chicago, Ill. ,to take charge of the Plankinton, which was little better then than a country tavern. Everything was conducted in the simplest and most crude way, but Mr. Miles had confidence in the growing West. To give some idea of the Plankinton at that time, it may be mentioned that the tables were of the old-fashioned extension type, covered with red table cloths, which were washed once a week; cold plates for hot meals were placed on the table before the doors were opened; tenderloin steaks were served only to men of note; such relishes as cucumbers, lettuce, radishes, celery, etc.,

J. J. MILES.

Headwaiter, The Plankinton Hotel, Milwaukee, Wis.

were not heard of out of season and were considered as luxuries; the chinaware was of the coarsest and heaviest white material; soup tureens and coffee pots were unknown.

Under the progressive management and magic hand of Mr. Miles the Plankinton is to-day the twentieth century hotel of the West, the Waldorf-Astoria of Milwaukee. There is only one guest remaining in the hotel who was there when Mr. Miles took charge—Mr. George W. Mitchell.

In this hotel the heads of the various departments are kept busy every day concocting plans and improvements for the comfort of their patrons and to meet the progressive ideas of the age in which we are living. It is progress all the time at the Plankinton, and that Mr. Miles has held his position for over a quarter of a century is the greatest tribute which the proprietors can pay to his sterling worth, and it speaks more eloquently than any pen can portray of the business qualities of the man. Mr. Miles is a firm believer in the European plan. To quote his own words: "In all my experience I have found nothing that comes up to my ideal of economy, like the hotel managed exclusively on the European plan."

Mr. Miles' biography ought to be an instructive lesson to young men of the reward which will surely come to a life of earnest endeavor and conscientious attention to duty.

Headwaiter *(Deceased)*.

THOMAS FRAZIER.

Thomas Frazier, the late head waiter of the Chittenden Hotel, Columbus, Ohio, was born in Charleston, S. C., in 1852, and died on the 15th of June, 1903.

By his death the young men of the present generation have lost a true friend. Mr. Frazier did everything in his power to stimulate the young men with whom he came in contact, for he was a firm believer in the efficacy of good example and good advice. Knowing the conditions which militate against the young man of color, he made much allowance for many of the frailties found in the people of his race. He believed that a great deal of the shortcomings is the result of the lack of home influence, proper training and encouragement in their efforts to better their condition. He was able to win the confidence and respect of all with whom he came in contact, and he took great pleasure in directing the efforts of all who came under his influence.

He was a man of domestic habits and his family relations were exceedingly happy.

His career in the hotel business was a very successful one. Among the most prominent hotels at which he was head waiter, may be mentioned, the Kimball, Atlanta, Ga.; Hotel Portland, Portland, Ore.; Endicott, New York City; Great Northern, Chicago, Ill.; Leland Hotel, Springfield, Ill.; Hotel Indian River, Rockledge, Fla.; Leon Hotel, Tallahassee, Fla.; Hot Springs Hotel, Hot Springs, N. C.; Ocean House, Newport, R. I.; The World's Inn, Chicago, Ill.; Great Southern, Columbus, Ohio; Hanover, Philadelphia, Pa.; Gladstone, Narragansett Pier, and the New Grand Hotel, Catskills, New York.

He was a member of the Head and Second Waiters' National Benefit Association, and his absence will be greatly felt at the meetings of this organization.

SAMUEL THOMPSON,
Headwaiter, Harrisburg, Pa.

SAMUEL THOMPSON.

The subject of this sketch, Mr. Samuel Thompson, was born in the city of Westminster, in the State of Maryland, on the 5th day of October, 1845. His parents were David and Mary Jane Thompson.

Like a great many others to whom fortune has been unkind, Mr. Thompson was deprived of the opportunity of a liberal education, and was forced to enter life with only that general knowledge gained by instinctive observation in the world's great theatre of general activity. But, it is more than likely that had this individual character been favored with an opportunity to acquire that educational force which tends to expand and develop the mind, and sets in action those natural instincts with which a Divine Creator has endowed all men—some in a larger, others in a smaller degree—he would to-day have been found occupying a place among the most influential of the leaders of his race.

It was at the Lochiel Hotel, under Mr. Samuel Bennett, in the year 1865, that Mr. Thompson first entered the hotel calling, and notwithstanding the fact that he was greatly handicapped because of his scant education, he has by the natural forces within him, gone through the various grades of the hotel calling, and for upwards of 30 years has been gradually making his way onward and upward.

During these 30 years of service, Mr. Thompson has served in various capacities in many of the large and leading houses throughout the country. It was at the Bolton, however, that he took his first charge as a head waiter.

Mr. Thompson belongs to that class of men to whom success in any undertaking is certain. He believes in pushing forward steadily, and in using every honest and available means in accomplishing the desired end, being convinced that whatever is to come to him, must come through the improvement of every moment, the acceptance of every opportunity, and the strict and conscientious application to duty.

He is blessed with a small, but happy family, and enjoys the happiness afforded in the gift of an only daughter.

Mr. Thompson is also a member of the Head, Second and Side Waiters' National Benefit Association.

GEORGE P. GOODE,

Ass't. Headwaiter, the new St. Charles, New Orleans, La.

GEO. P. GOODE.

The subject of this sketch, Mr. George P. Goode, was born in Columbus, S. C., where he received his education and spent the early part of his life.

Like many other young men whose history adorns the pages of this work, Mr. Goode, after completing his education, became imbued with the desire to better his condition, and thus directed his attention towards the North, which is regarded by many as the theatre of greatest activity, and where it is believed the opportunities are more numerous; and so in 1890 he arrived in New York City.

It can be said of Mr. Goode that he started from the very bottom of his calling; but as will be seen, it was not very long before, by the exercise of his natural ability and keen perception, he was able to reach the top.

His first employment in New York City was as a bell boy, and in this capacity he served in many of the well-known hotels along Broadway, and other parts of the city during the winter months; going, during the summer seasons to some of the various summer resorts.

Having a natural aptitude for his calling, and being possessed of more than ordinary ability with marked politeness, he was able to master the minute details of the dining room with such rapidity that in 1893, just three years after reaching New York, he was appointed second waiter in the Mansion House, Brooklyn, N. Y., a house whose reputation is well-known. It was at this place that Dame Fortune was pleased to place her crown of highest reward upon the head of Mr. Goode, for in the following year, he became head waiter, and the successor of Mr. James Mayhew.

It was about this time, also, that Mr. Goode took charge of the United States Hotel, at Long Branch, during the summer, and which place he held until 1898.

In the summer of this year, Mr. Goode accepted the position of second waiter at the Sagamore Hotel, Lake George, under Mr. Frank Griffin. Leaving the Sagamore, he returned to Brooklyn, and there assumed charge of the Pierrepont House, as head waiter. For the past four seasons Mr. Goode has been in charge of the dining room department of the Kensington House, Saratoga, N. Y., as head waiter.

and as second waiter at the new St. Charles Hotel, New Orleans, La., under Mr. G. A. Curry, and at which place he is at present.

Thus it is that Mr. Goode, starting out with a desire to succeed in his calling, did not have very long to wait for his reward. His earnestness of purpose led him on inspiringly to the goal of his ambition. His rapid success, resulting from his steadfastness of purpose, politeness and congeniality, is an evidence of what can be accomplished by the exercise of the right principles, and should act as a happy inspiration to other young men in this, as well as many other callings.

EDWARD F. MATHEWS.

Edward F. Mathews was born in Chillicothe, Ohio, on November 7th, 1873. It was there that he received his education, and even in his school days gave evidence of extraordinary ability. He was 6 years of age when he entered school, and at the age of 15 had completed his common school studies, and entered the high school. On entering the high school, young Mathews found himself the only one of his race attending that school. Here he completed three successful terms, and would have graduated in June of the same year, but having a desire for a business education, he left the school in February, and entered the Canton Business College at 90 Euclid avenue, Cleveland, Ohio, which at that time was managed by a very studious young man, Mr. H. T. Edmiston, also of Chillicothe, Ohio, and which college was regarded as the most prosperous institution of learning of its kind in Cleveland.

The principal studies taken up in this college by young Mathews were stenography and typewriting, and after 8 months' work, he was recommended by the president, Mr. M. J. Caton, for a position as stenographer with the Swasenberg Scrap Iron concern, where he remained for one year. Finding that this position was not remunerative enough, Mr. Mathews resigned, and accepted a place in the Hollenden Café as a waiter, under W. H. Kinney, who was then head waiter. At this time the Hollenden was considered among the employees as a rich mine for the gathering up of "tips," and so Mr. Mathews became wedded to the place, for he says "the dimes and quarters came rolling along in succession towards me."

Though engaged in hotel work chiefly on the European plan, he has never given up his practice in stenography and typewriting.

After he had spent four years at the Hollenden Café, going to Atlantic City during the summer months, Head Waiter Kinney engaged him, together with some others, to take charge of the Hotel Lincoln, in Pittsburg, which was considered one of the finest European houses in the city of Pittsburg. There Mr. Mathews and his associates succeeded white waiters. After serving in the Lincoln for two years, he was engaged by Mr. W. R. Harris, to work for the Bailey Catering Co., at the Pan-American Exposition, as one of the

EDWARD F. MATHEWS,
Assistant Headwaiter, Lincoln Hotel, Pittsburg, Pa.

Captains on the floor, and from that time Mr. Mathews' career as an officer began.

Immediately at the close of the Pan-American Exposition, Mr. Mathews was engaged by Mr. G. A. Baker, proprietor of the Tod House, Youngstown, Ohio, to take charge of a new café which he was about to open. For a time the café flourished, and the business continued to increase, until it became difficult to handle it; all this time young Mathews was gaining more and more experience, and making the acquaintance of some of the very best people in the city.

Consequently the increased knowledge gained and the large list of friends and acquaintances which Mr. Mathews made during this time, induced him, after a few months, to join issue with Mr. W. H. Kinney, and together they started a business enterprise for themselves, known as "The Youngstown Catering Co." This business flourished, and is to-day regarded as one of the most prosperous catering companies in the entire city.

In 1903, May 30th, he resigned his position at the café, to accept the head waitership of that wealthy club known as the Youngstown Club. Mr. Mathews did not remain here very long, however, owing to disagreements arising between himself and the steward, so in the following September he resigned his position and returned as head waiter at the Tod Café, where he remained until its close.

Mr. Mathews is a strong advocate of the European service, and expresses a happy desire to see such a change among the many hotels which are now being conducted upon the American plan.

The business ability and advanced ideas as evidenced by the career of Mr. Mathews, seems to foreshadow a very successful and fortunate future for him.

A. H. DAILEY,
Headwaiter, Blandensburg, Md.

A. H. DAILEY.

A. H. Dailey started as a waiter in a house conducted on the European plan, and after serving in many cafés and hotels as a side waiter, gradually worked his way to the top of the ladder. He earned his claim to be ranked as one of the most competent head waiters of the Capitol City, from the reputation he gained as a caterer while serving those artistic dinners which only Washington society can boast of.

He served as second waiter at the following hotels: The Colonial, of York Springs, Pa.; the Buena Vista Hotel, Buena Vista Springs, Md.; Hotel McClellan, Gettysburg, Pa.; Deer Park Hotel, Deer Park, Md. Being successful while serving in this capacity, Mr. Dailey's abilities were soon recognized, and when he applied for the head waitership of the Takoma Hotel, at Takoma Springs, Md., his application was accepted in preference to scores of others. Here he remained for two seasons, after which the proprietors of the Cairo Hotel, Washington, D. C., made him a satisfactory offer to superintend the dining rooms of this first-class house. Mr. Dailey felt he could not refuse this manifestation of the appreciation in which he was held by the hotel fraternity, and, therefore, accepted the position. While at this hotel, he firmly established himself as one of the factors in the control of the dining room of one of the largest hotels in the country, and also demonstrated his ability to handle a large force of men.

On leaving the Cairo he went to the Fredonia Hotel, but had been there but a short time when Col. O. G. Staples, of the Riggs House, Washington, D. C., learning of his proficiency as a caterer, sought him out and offered him the superintendency of his house, a place known throughout the District of Columbia, and to all the public men of the country, as the ideal place to enjoy a sumptuous repast. Mr. Staples wanted a capable man for the position, and found such a one in Mr. Dailey.

During the winter of 1902-03, Mr. Dailey resigned from the Riggs House, and returned to the Fredonia.

As an evidence of the appreciation in which Mr. Dailey was held by those who had once employed him, after going back to the Fredonia, he was again approached and induced to return to the Riggs House, at which place he has remained ever since.

There are men whose lives have been so even and regular that they are unable to narrate any stirring event, which has happened in their lives. These are the real plodders, and the men who show results.

In this life the old adage "A rolling stone gathers no moss," bears its impression of truth, for the world is not moved by such men; but the men who concentrate their energies and efforts in any given point, and who persistently and steadily go forward towards the accomplishment of their purpose, these are the men who finally succeed. It is to this class of men that Mr. Dailey belongs.

FRANK C. LONG.

F. C. Long, head waiter at the Windermere Hotel, Chicago, Ill., was born February 12th, 1865, in Hillsboro, N. C. He began his career as a waiter in the McAdoo House, Greensboro, N. C., from which place he went to the Arlington, thence to the Ebbitt, and from there to the Wormsley Hotel, Washington, D. C. Since he became a head waiter he has been employed at the head of the dining room department in some of the leading hotels at Saratoga, Shelter Island, N. Y.; New London, Conn.; St. Joseph, Mich., and was four seasons at the Hotel Marrogate, Tennessee, five years at the Milliard Hotel, Omaha, Neb.; also a number of years at the Colonial Hotel, Cleveland, Ohio, from which he went to the Windermere, Chicago, and after serving three years there, he resigned to take charge of the Gayoso Hotel, Memphis, Tenn. At this hotel he succeeded a white head waiter, and had under his command a crew of 50 waiters of his own selection. He gave ample satisfaction there. At the end of four months' service, however, he received a very liberal offer from his old employer at the Windermere, Chicago, which induced him to return to that hotel, at which place he still is, having been given *carte blanche* of the dining room.

Mr. Long is acknowledged to be one of the best head waiters in the country, and is now receiving the highest salary ever paid to a colored head waiter in the city of Chicago; besides the hotel furnishes him a suite of rooms with bath, and boards him and his wife.

The Windermere is the best and finest family hotel in Chicago, and employs a crew of twenty-five waiters, at a salary of $25 per month and room.

Color is no bar at the Windermere. Mr. Long's table is alongside that of the manager and one of the night clerks is a colored man, promoted from the bell stand.

Mr. Long is one of the originators of the Head and Second Waiters' Association, in fact, it was he who first sounded the key note of the necessity of such an association. In 1897 Mr. Long contributed an article to the *Hotel World*, entitled "The Modern Head Waiter," in which he said in part: "The chief weakness among

FRANK C. LONG,

Headwaiter, Hotel Windermere, Chicago, Ill.; Ex-Treasurer and ex-Vice-President, Head and Second Waiters' National Benefit Assn.

head waiters of to-day is that they know so little about each other. There is no fraternity among them, their knowledge is not imparted one to the other, as is the case with the stewards and chefs.

"Every head waiter will agree that the spirit of fraternity should be more largely fostered, and an opportunity given for a comparison and exchange of ideas. Each one then being alert for new methods could impart them to their less fortunate brothers, and the best systems, rules and regulations could be discussed, thus insuring a larger measure of success for everyone so engaged. The question of a strong fraternity is worthy the serious consideration of every head waiter. They should weld themselves into a bond of mutual union and work with hands, head and heart to ennoble their calling, so that in the closing years of the nineteenth century the head waiters will be abreast of the times."

In a later article to the *Hotel World*, entitled, "Head Waiters' Association," Mr. Long said, in part: "In my article of April 22, the question of a national head waiters' association was incidentally referred to and recommended.

"Since the issuance of the above publication I have received a number of letters from several of our leading head waiters, touching the subject and endorsing the same. The time, therefore, seems opportune for the further discussion of this matter, and for the presentation of plans and lines along which this dream may bud forth into a living and beneficent reality."

After outlining his plans and advising that all questions of wages should be left for the individual employer and employee to settle and for the banishment of unionism. Mr. Long said, in conclusion: "Every head waiter should take this matter under serious consideration, and begin to look toward the formation of such an organization. It is the crying need of the hour, it is imperative that we should be panoplied with the benefits of mutual fraternity, and thus keep abreast with the times."

In accordance with the above, a committee of nine was organized, with W. F. Cozart as Chairman; T. C. Long, Treasurer, and J. B. Goins, Secretary. This committee formulated plans and called the first convention to meet in Chicago, September 21, 1899, at which time Mr. Long was made Vice-President for the State of Ohio.

MARION M. MARTIN,
Headwaiter, on Steamboat *Pilgrim*, Fall River Line.

MARION M. MARTIN.

Marion M. Martin was born in Richmond, Va., May 15, 1856. His parents later moved to Lincoln, N. C., and settled on a little farm of their own. Thus, young Marion, the subject of this sketch, began life as a farmer on his father's farm, where he worked for a period of nine years. Even at this early age he manifested marked ability in the mastery of minute details and a steadiness of purpose, seldom found in a youth of his age. After nine years of service on the farm, he decided that the area of the farm was too contracted, and the knowledge to be gained there, too limited for his ambition; he, therefore, left the farm and secured work in a tobacco factory. In this factory he labored for several years and was promoted from one department to another. Finally he accepted a government position as an inspector of tobacco in that district, owing to his expert knowledge of tobacco. This position he held until the factory closed. Not finding anything immediately after this to do, he entered the Pullman service and railroaded for seven years. Becoming tired of this employment, he gave it up and followed hotel waiting. After serving on the side with superior ability, in many of the leading hotels in the State of Virginia, and passing through the various grades in the calling, he reached the position of a dining room superintendent. His first position as such was at the American Hotel, Richmond, Va., in 1878.

Since that time he has served as head waiter of the St. Charles, Richmond, Va.; the Greenbrier, White Sulphur Springs, W. Va.; Old Sweet Springs, Rockbridge Alum Springs, Va.; the Hot Springs, Hot Springs, Va.

Believing he could better his condition in the North, he left the Hot Springs and came to New York. In 1895 he entered the service of the Old Colony Co., now known as the New York, New Haven & Hartford R. R. Co., and has ever since been in the service of this company. Entering the service as a side waiter, although he had been head of the dining room of several large hotels, and had given ample satisfaction, he soon rose to the head of the service, and is to-day the leading head waiter in the company's employ. He is at present head waiter of the steamboat *Pilgrim* on the Fall River line, and has served on every boat, and on every line operated by the company; some time as steward of one of the smaller boats. He is a man of very steady habits, and loves his humble fireside, where he finds always to cheer him an amiable wife whom he married twenty-four years ago. He is blessed with one son who is following in his footsteps.

Mr. Martin is not only an efficient dining room superintendent, but one of the most progressive men in the calling. He possesses also much ability as an artist in wax work. At times, when not engaged in his regular calling, he has made upwards of fifty dollars per week by working out different designs in wax. He has, however, been compelled to abandon this work on account of its affecting his eyes. This artistic ability he demonstrated at a very early age, as will be seen from the following extract taken from an evening paper, printed in Charlotte, N. C., December 25, 1876: "At the hotels, extra fine dinners were served and the guests were numerous. At the Central the dining room was kept open from 1:30 to 4:30 o'clock, and the finest dinners that has ever been known in Charlotte was spread before the guests. The Buford House also made an extra effort and had a superb bill of fare. On a center table was a representation of the Brooklyn Bridge surrounded by Christmas trees, on which were perched birds made from cake and soaps, flowers from vegetables, etc., the work of Marion M. Martin, one of the waiters."

F. H. GRIFFIN.

In the progress of mankind the individual pushes out on the ocean of life for himself, inspired with a determination to reach a harbor of success, and thus the aggregate success of the individual makes the sum total of human progress.

While it has been said of many others that they have been successful, in the case of Mr. F. H. Griffin, it must be said that as a commander of the dining room, he has been eminently successful.

Mr. Griffin was born in Savannah, Ga., in 1864. He commenced his hotel career in 1877 as a side waiter, and served for years in many of the first-class hotels, such as The Brunswick and Youngs in Boston, the Stuyvesant and Rossmore of New York City.

In 1886 he took his first charge as a head waiter of the McSparan Hotel, Narragansett Pier, and held the same for four seasons. Leaving there, he went to the St. Clair Hotel, Green Cove Springs, Fla. He superintended the dining room of this hotel for one season, and from there went to the Crocker House, New London, Conn., where he remained another season. From there he went to the Hotel Bon Air, Summerville Heights, Augusta, Ga. At this place he remained for seven seasons. Giving up this house, he accepted the command of the Hotel Castleton, New Brighton, Staten Island, N. Y. At this hotel, Mr. Griffin made a magnificent record, filling the position for three seasons. He then went to the Kenilworth Inn, Asheville, N. C., where he remained for two seasons; at the end of which he went to the Piney Woods Hotel, Thomasville, Ga., where he served for four seasons. On resigning his position there, he took charge of the Sagamore Hotel, Lake George, N. Y., and has been at this hotel for a period of eleven years. Mr. Griffin is also head waiter of the Hampton Terrace, North Augusta, Aiken County, S. C., at which place he has served two seasons superintending the dining room of the Sagamore in the spring and summer, and the Hampton Terrace during the fall and winter months.

Mr. Griffin is a very progressive man and no doubt will still rise to greater heights of success, for he is possessed of steady habits and eminent business ability.

F. H. GRIFFIN,
Headwaiter, Sagamore Hotel, Lake George, N. Y. and Hampton Terrace, North Augusta, Aiken Co., S. C.

ROBERT JAMES PATTERSON.

R. J. Patterson, the son of William H. and Laura F. (Page) Patterson, was born September 1st, 1869, at Lynchburg, Va. He attended the public schools in his native city from the time he was seven years of age, until he was fourteen. When nine years of age he commenced the sale of newspapers, and continued in this until he left school. After he left school, he secured employment as a porter on a railroad, where he remained for two years. In 1885 he left the road and journeyed to the North. On reaching New York, he entered the service of the Old Colony Company on one of its steamboats running between New York and Fall River, and has continued in this service from that time up to the present, working his way up from the bottom to the top of his calling, and is to-day the efficient superintendent of the dining room of the palatial steamboat *Priscilla*, having risen to the position of head of the dining room several years ago.

He is one of the most popular employees in the company's service, and is very much liked by his employers and the guests, as well as by the men who serve under him. While he is a strict disciplinarian, he always treats his men with fairness and consideration. He is thoroughly conversant with all the little niceties that go to make up an attractive dining room. He retains a calmness of temperament at all times, and whether the dining room is filled to the utmost capacity or whether it has but few, Mr. Patterson's coolness of disposition remains the same.

In 1894 Mr. Patterson decided that a bachelor was only part of what the Creator intended a man should be, and therefore determined to settle down. Finding his ideal in the person of Miss Galamina Valentine, of Guttenburg, N. J., he became united in marriage and resigned himself to the affectionate government of a loving wife.

Although making their home in the city of Fall River, they have purchased a very fine piece of property in Hoboken, N. J.

That Mr. Patterson is an able man in his calling is self-evident. To be in the continuous employ of a company whose patrons are so numerous and consist of all classes, for the number of years he has been, and to have risen from the bottom to the top of the service, prove the ability, sagacity and integrity of the man.

ROBERT JAMES PATTERSON,
Headwaiter on Steamboat *Priscilla*, Fall River Line.

EDWARD WILSON DIGGS.

The success of the individual is due mainly to the efforts he puts forth, and his ability, to correctly grasp conditions and to utilize, to its greatest capacity, the force of circumstances that surround him. Imbued with the idea of these facts the young man of whom we write started out in life, and has been pressing onward steadily.

December 25th, 1873, Edward W. Diggs was born in Southampton County, Va. He attended school until he was 12 years of age. On leaving school he went to Norfolk, Va., and entered the employ of a hotel as fireman. From fireman he rose to bellman, and later was promoted to the position of head bellman.

In 1889 he left Norfolk and went to Philadelphia where he secured employment in a private family with whom he remained until 1893, during the fall, winter and spring months, and worked as a waiter in some of the leading hotels in Atlantic City, Asbury Park and Long Branch during the summer months of this period.

He got his first official position as a head waiter in 1892 at the Buena Vista Hotel, Ocean Grove, N. J.

In the spring of 1893, he went to Europe, visiting: England, Ireland, France, Germany, Belgium, Italy and many other countries on the Continent in the capacity of valet to Mr. F. T. Leach, of Philadelphia. He returned to the U. S. in the fall of the same year, and settled down in Boston, where he got employment in the United States Hotel. In the fall of 1894 he came to New York City and engaged in service with a private family. During the summer of '95 he went to Cape May, N. J., as second waiter at the Hotel Chalfonte, and from thence to Philadelphia. The season of 1896 he went to the Ocean House, Newport, and from there he went with Mr. Thomas Fraizer to Columbus, Ohio, and opened the Great Southern, as secretary and second waiter. He served as captain at the Windsor, Cape May, in 1897, and as head waiter at the Marine Hotel the same place, from 1898 to the close of the season of 1900. He then went as second waiter to the St. Charles, Atlantic City. On leaving Atlantic City he came to New York, and entered the employ of the Fall River Line as second waiter under R. J. Patterson, on the *Priscilla,* from which he was later transferred to the *Plymouth* as head waiter on the Providence Line, where he still is.

EDWARD W. DIGGS,
Headwaiter on Steamboat *Plymouth*, Providence Line,

W. FORREST COZART.

Winfield Forrest Cozart was born October 14th, 1867. He commenced his hotel career at the age of twelve, and at twenty-one became a head waiter. Since then he has been in charge of some of the largest hotels in the East.

At the summit of his success as a dining room superintendent, after having given much study to the art of first-class waiting, he wrote the *Waiter's Manual,* in 1897, the first book of its kind ever published. In 1898 he established a Waiter's Column in the Indianapolis *Freeman.* As a man of much thought and action, Mr. Cozart is always endeavoring to advance the interest of the men in the calling, and thus it was that in 1899, himself and others founded the Head and Second Waiters' National Benefit Association. He was elected the first president of this association and received a re-election at the second convention held in Pittsburg, Pa. Press of business, however, caused him to resign. At the convention held at Buffalo, N. Y., in 1901, he was chosen to respond to the address of welcome to the association delivered by the mayor of that city.

Mr. Cozart has been a prolific writer on matters pertaining to the dining room, and at one time, was special correspondent for the *Hotel World,* Chicago, Ill.; a position he held for seven years. His articles were very often quoted by some of the leading journals and received high commendation. He is a high authority not only on good waiting, but on the etiquette of guests in the dining room.

After a successful career as a commander in many of the leading hotel dining rooms, and having much experience in journalism, he has settled down to literary work, and is now the editor and publisher of the *State Register,* at Atlantic City, N. J.

In appreciation and recognition of the many efforts to better the condition of the men in the calling, Mr. Leland M. Fisher, one of the coming negro poets, dedicated the following poem to Mr. Cozart:

>Here's to you, Cozart, God bless you!
>Here's to you forever and aye.
>Here's hoping that care may not press you;
>Here are blossoms and blessings of May.
>
>When life's path downward is sloping
>May the sky that bends o'er you keep blue,
>While song birds warble your praises,
>'Mid flowers, wild wet with the dew.

W. Forrest Cozart,
Atlantic City, N. J.
1st Pres. of Head, Second and Side Waiters' National Benefit Association.

SOUTHERN FOODWAYS ALLIANCE
STUDIES IN CULTURE, PEOPLE, AND PLACE

The Larder: Food Studies Methods from the American South
   edited by John T. Edge, Elizabeth Engelhardt, and Ted Ownby

Hog Meat and Hoecake: Food Supply in the Old South, 1840–1860
   by Sam Bowers Hilliard

To Live and Dine in Dixie: The Evolution of Urban Food Culture in the Jim Crow South
   by Angela Jill Cooley

Still Hungry in America
   photography by Al Clayton; text by Robert Coles; introduction by Edward M. Kennedy; with a new foreword by Thomas J. Ward Jr.

Catfish Dream: Ed Scott's Fight for His Family Farm and Racial Justice in the Mississippi Delta
   by Julian Rankin

Creole Italian: Sicilian Immigrants and the Shaping of New Orleans Food Culture
   by Justin A. Nystrom

Recipes for Respect: African American Meals and Meaning
   by Rafia Zafar

Commanders of the Dining Room: Biographic Sketches and Portraits of Successful Head Waiters
   by E. A. Maccannon